Breakthrough

Breakthrough

A Growth Revolution

Martin Fleming

BUSINESS EXPERT PRESS

Leader in applied, concise business books

Breakthrough: A Growth Revolution

Copyright © Business Expert Press, LLC, 2023.

Cover design by Kostis Pavlou

Interior design by Exeter Premedia Services Private Ltd., Chennai, India

First published in 2022 by
Business Expert Press, LLC
222 East 46th Street, New York, NY 10017
www.businessexpertpress.com

ISBN-13: 978-1-63742-309-7 (paperback)
ISBN-13: 978-1-63742-310-3 (e-book)

Business Expert Press Collaborative Intelligence Collection

First edition: 2022

10 9 8 7 6 5 4 3 2 1

Description

What's necessary for the United States and other developed nations to realize stronger growth and more equal incomes? What's necessary for families to feel vacations, college educations, and retirements are possible? Will artificial intelligence (AI) automate or augment workers' jobs? Will the 2020–2021 global pandemic be sufficiently disruptive to deliver fundamental transformation?

The growth dynamics of the developed economies experience significant variation over long periods. This book examines the economic logic of such variation and whether the long-term movement is the result of random events or whether improved outcomes arise from within the system.

To explore these questions, the Fourth Industrial Revolution is a unique frame to assess global economic transformation in the decades ahead. The industrial revolution framework provides a point-in-time reference for placing current events in the context of sustained, multidecade periods of faster or slower GDP and productivity growth. Political, social, and economic metamorphoses have accompanied each revolution.

In each revolution, a new general-purpose technology, such as information technology, initially gives rise to "mushroom" growth with scattered success popping up, while latter "yeasty" growth takes hold with economic activity leavened by increased capital investment, education, skills, knowledge transfer, technology diffusion, and labor income share.

Successful economic performance in the decades ahead will depend on whether households, businesses, and governments are willing to alter behavior, engage in innovation, achieve improved balance between traditional and nontraditional values and beliefs, and respond to pressures to bring about a future of more rapid growth and more equal income distribution.

Energy technology evolution will address the climate change and global warming consequences of fossil-fuel technologies and, if successful, over the long-term result in renewable energy sources, reducing energy expense.

The book proposes a growth and fairness agenda through which stronger economic growth and more equally distributed incomes can be possible.

- Recognize traditional policy actions may be insufficient to achieve stronger long-term growth.
- Promote improved confidence and a positive outlook among small and medium enterprises.
- Encourage advances in AI technology while addressing risks and fairness issues.
- Support deeper worker engagement between business leaders and workers.
- Seek a new social contract among workers, businesses, and governments.

Keywords

growth revolution; fairness; equality; new social contract; income distribution; wage increase; worker engagement; small and medium business; Fourth Industrial Revolution; Artificial Intelligence; capital investment; tangible investment; intangible assets; growth dynamics; general-purpose technology; knowledge diffusion; absorptive capacity; labor income share; capital income share

Contents

List of Figures

List of Tables

Testimonials

"Martin Fleming lays out a road map for hope. He sees the potential and a way to overcome some of our largest economic hurdles."—**Diane Swonk, KPMG, Chief Economist**

"Martin Fleming has written an engaging and important book that identifies actionable pathways for inclusive growth in the post-pandemic recovery. A must-read for anyone interested in our economic future."—**Susan Lund, Vice President, Economics and Private Sector Development, International Finance Corporation, World Bank Group**

"Martin Fleming has penned an outstanding book, laying out the dynamics of the ongoing AI-industrial revolution. It deserves reading by a wide audience of economists, policymakers, analysts, and students, across disciplines."—**Stuart P.M. Mackintosh, Executive Director, Group of Thirty**

Foreword

Over five decades, the developed world has experienced the great inflation, the great moderation, the great recession, the jobless recovery, secular stagnation, a savings glut, and a "once in a century pandemic" among other crises and economic events. Through it all, economic growth, productivity growth, and capital investment have remained disappointingly weak. The advent of a stream of new digital technologies, a wide array of fiscal and monetary policy actions, and a broad set of new worker skills, all have failed to compensate for economic volatility. The fear is that employment and incomes are threatened by the impact of artificial intelligence (AI) automating workers' jobs.

The Productivity Institute was created by the UK government to bring together scholars, business leaders, and policy makers to consider these challenges and explore what productivity means for businesses, workers, and communities—how it is measured and how it truly contributes to increased living standards and well-being. The aspiration is to contribute to improved outcomes in terms of productivity and more inclusive economic development, not only in the United Kingdom but also across the entire developed world.

Already the institute's work has focused on how a longer-term perspective and a decentralization of public policy could provide benefits broadly across income groups and regions. The institute's work has also looked at how heightened uncertainty, following the 2020–2021 global pandemic in combination with supply chain disruption, labor shortages, and rising costs, has impacted the business sector, public policy, and household decisions in regard to investment and economic activity. Can crises force more agility and resilience?

In *Breakthrough: A Growth Revolution,* Martin Fleming confronts these challenges and provides a long view of economic activity to consider the growth dynamics of developed economies. The book examines the economic logic of the variation in growth performance over two centuries and whether the long-term movement is the result of random events or whether improved outcomes arise from within the economic system. To explore these questions, the Fourth Industrial Revolution provides a unique frame to assess global economic transformation in the decades ahead.

Building on decades of scholarship, Fleming defines an industrial revolution as the economic and social transformation occurring as a result of the lengthy and complex interaction of capital investment, technological change, and creative destruction along with the redefinition of how work gets done and how businesses are organized. Over the course of an industrial revolution, investment in machinery, equipment, and intellectual property can shift from substituting for the skill of workers to complementing the skill of workers. Industrial revolutions create the need for new worker skills to build, deploy, and use the new technology, as well as time to adjust to the new social norms implied by the revolutionary transformation.

Each industrial revolution brings amazing and previously inconceivable technological advances that drive unimagined innovation in business, work, and life. Industrial revolution shifts activity from an existing legacy era to a new era dominated by new technology and new capital investment. But new business models and new ways of working are as much the essence of industrial revolution as is technology, innovation, and creative destruction. Importantly, industrial revolution transforms economies to unequal degrees, shifting the nature of the competition for wealth among nations.

In each revolution, a general-purpose technology, such as the new digital technology, initially gives rise to "mushroom" growth with scattered success popping up with firms and sectors. Knowledge diffusion and absorptive capacity is limited as firms at technology's leading edge attract the necessary skill, engage in innovative activity, and achieve early success. The successful innovators become industry superstars with new technology rapidly appearing.

With maturing technology, business models transform, and a new regime emerges, bringing much greater knowledge diffusion and deeper absorptive capacity across a much wider universe of firms. "Yeasty" growth takes hold with economic activity leavened by increased capital investment, education, and skills. With stronger economic and productivity growth, labor demand strengthens, and labor's income share begins to climb.

As the technology simplifies and a broader set of firms absorb the new technology, success requires that workers see their interest in gaining new skills, transforming practices, and changing behavior. With AI, the new digital technology is especially meaningful in services sectors, where worker engagement is critically important in determining service delivery quality. Worker engagement—and the service quality it allows—is a result of workers' skills, satisfaction, career paths, and compensation. More engaged workers are more productive and, thus, better compensated and supported in their careers. With services sectors continuing in importance in the period ahead, worker engagement will take on added significance as a broad set of firms absorb the newly available technology and business models. Creative destruction and transformation will be widespread.

Successful economic performance in the decades ahead, according to Fleming, will depend on whether households, businesses, and governments are willing to alter their behaviors, engage in innovation, achieve improved balance between traditional and nontraditional values and beliefs, and respond to pressures to bring about a future of more rapid growth and more equal income distribution.

Fleming is also careful to point out that there are topics such as shifting demographics and China's emergence in the global economy after a century and a half of relative quiescence that have not been fully explored. There is also the big elephant in the room of economic growth, which is climate change. If the Fourth Industrial Revolution is to successfully improve economic outcomes, energy technology evolution will be required to address the climate change and global warming consequences of fossil-fuel technologies. If successful, over the long term, such a transformation will result in renewable energy sources, reducing energy expense.

Fleming does not assume or predict the success of the Fourth Industrial Revolution. Rather, he focuses on the conditions necessary, and the actions required for the realization of benefits comparable to those of earlier periods. More robust economic and productivity growth along with improved income distribution are very possible but change, transformation, and creative destruction will certainly be necessary. To realize a more satisfying future, Fleming proposes a Growth and Fairness Agenda through which stronger economic growth and more equally distributed incomes can be possible.

—Bart van Ark,
Managing Director,
The Productivity Institute

Preface

The Fourth Industrial Revolution continues to receive attention from a wide array of business leaders, investors, and senior public officials. To date, deep work has been largely limited to Karl Schwab and the World Economic Forum. Among economists, industrial revolution has been a central concept in the work of economic historians as 250 years of progress has been explored, most notably the 18th and 19th centuries' industrial revolutions. However, among economists, not working in economic history, industrial revolution has received little attention. Consequently, the use of an industrial revolution framework as an analytical device is a novel contribution.

The purpose of this book is to understand the growth dynamics experienced across the developed economies over long periods. This book examines the economic logic of such variation—the economic, social, and political forces underlying the variation—and whether the long-term movement is the result of random events or whether improved outcomes arise from within the system. The short answer is that there is some of both. Understanding the economics of long-term growth and using an industrial revolution framework, a view of the conditions required to bring about a future of stronger growth with more equal income distribution may be possible. Imagining a more prosperous future begins with an understanding of the successes and failures of the past.

Acknowledgments

This book would never have been possible without the strong interest and encouragement of Bart van Ark, the managing director of The Productivity Institute. Bart has been a friend and colleague for nearly two decades. Bart has given his time generously and read carefully the paper that was the basis of this book. Bart has encouraged and supported the book project over its entire recent journey. My long-time friend and former IBM colleague, Jim Spohrer, watched this work grow and mature over many years. Perhaps it shouldn't be surprising that Jim quickly came across the original paper on The Productivity Institute website and, in his role as a Business Expert Press editor, encouraged me to expand the paper into a book and join the Business Expert Press family. Jim's comments on the manuscript are much appreciated.

Diane Coyle of the University of Cambridge also read the original paper in detail and provided valuable comments. The book and my work are a better product after much long discussion with Tony Venables of the University of Oxford who patiently read much of my initial work. My friends and Conference of Business Economist colleagues, Diane Swonk, Chief Economist, KPMG; Stuart Mackintosh, Executive Director, The Group of Thirty; and Susan Lund, formerly, McKinsey and Company and now Vice President, Economics and Private Sector Development, International Finance Corporation, The World Bank, each read and commented on the manuscript.

In all intellectual endeavors, there is a long legacy that can hopefully bear fruit. Most recently David Autor and Daron Acemoglu of MIT, and Erik Brynjolfsson, now at Stanford University, have provided support in sharing their time and insight. Having spent 20 years at IBM, the last 10 of which as Chief Economist and Chief Analytics Officer, many friends and colleagues have influenced this work. The current work's origin finds its way back to the three years I spent in IBM's corporate strategy group, having been introduced to Carlota Perez and her work by Joel Cawley, Dan McGrath, and Bruce Harreld. Finally, having spent a year—many years ago—as a research assistant to Jay Forrester at MIT, I grew to appreciate the dynamics of complex systems along with, importantly, what it means to do quality work.

It has been a pleasure to have joined Varicent as Chief Revenue Scientist. Marc Altshuller, Varicent CEO, and Marcus Hearne, Chief Marketing Officer, have been supportive throughout this effort. The opportunity to both see and contribute to the innovation and deployment of new technology on a first-hand basis has been immeasurably helpful.

The publication process has been made relatively pain free due the effort of Scott Isenberg, Managing Executive Editor, and Charlene Kronstedt, Director Production and Marketing, both of Business Expert Press. My thanks go to both. David Yaun has provided important support in communicating this work to the broader world. Anna Sekaren has also provided her coaching and guidance.

As ever, the love and support of my wife, best friend, and partner, Patricia, has made it all possible. I am delighted to dedicate this book to her.

CHAPTER 1

Introduction

The Growth Revolution Ahead

Pandemics have plagued the world for centuries. While the 2020–2021 pandemic is often viewed as a time unlike any other, in fact, the current pandemic has joined a long history of global pandemics. Dating back 700 years, each has profoundly altered social and economic activity in the decades that followed (see Jordà, Singh, and Taylor 2020). The current pandemic will likely be very similar.

What gives the 2020–2021 pandemic a unique flavor is the very rapid appearance of life-saving science and technology delivering vaccines and antiviral drugs, limiting illness and death. The availability of a robust global technology network also uniquely allowed many to work from home and to shop in comfort, privacy, and safety.

But the current pandemic is also unique in that it appeared just as the global economy is poised to enter a period of robust growth, offering the possibility of both greater wealth and more equally distributed incomes. The pandemic-induced dislocation, which has inflicted widespread death and suffering, may very well accelerate the potential for a robust social and economic revival in the decades ahead. While the future is uncertain, if pressures arising from the pandemic compel business leaders, workers, families, and elected officials to transform behaviors, the global economy might very well breakthrough to an era of robust growth and more equally distributed incomes.

Stronger long-term growth is no small matter. Small year-to-year differences in economic growth can have large cumulative effects over the long term. Small improvements in tangible and intangible capital investment as well as productivity growth over decades and even centuries can potentially result in as much or more impact on economic growth as substantial living standard increases in the near term.

Political and business leaders have realized the opportunity for long-term growth and have recently begun framing the challenge in terms of the Fourth Industrial Revolution. President Biden remarked:

> This is a little bit not unlike what happened in 1932. There was a fundamental change, not only taking place here in the United States, but around the world. We're in the middle of the fourth industrial revolution where there's a real question of whether or not what—all the changes in technology. Will there be middle class? What will people be doing? … and there's genuine, genuine anxiety.[1]

Similarly, former Bank of England governor Mark Carney urged a reinvention of the central bank for the Fourth Industrial Revolution. Carney said: "We are on the cusp of a Fourth Industrial Revolution, which has the potential to transform fundamentally the nature of both work and commerce through advances in AI, automation and interconnectedness" (Carney 2018). However, the notion of a Fourth Industrial Revolution has received most attention from Klaus Schwab, the founder of the World Economic Forum (WEF). Schwab has written at length of the "profound and systemic change" expected. With a primary focus on leadership and technology, Schwab has encouraged the focus of the many exclusive and well-attended WEF annual sessions on the implications and impact arising from the "speed and breath of this new revolution" (Schwab 2016).

These leaders and others have felt compelled to react to two decades of disappointing growth, limited capital investment, low inflation, inexpensive credit, and a mysterious slowing in productivity improvement. Productivity growth has decelerated sharply from the rapid pace of the postwar decades of the 1950s, 1960s, and 1970s. After a brief revival in the 1990s, productivity growth across the developed world has slowed

---

[1] CNN Live Event/Special. Interview with President-Elect Joe Biden and Vice President-Elect Kamala Harris. Aired 9:00–10:00 PM ET, December 03, 2020.

once again in the decades of the early 21st century. With high investment levels and rapid trade expansion, emerging market economies likewise benefited from the 1990s rapid productivity improvement, only to also fall victim to the slowdown after the 1990s dot.com bubble and the 2008–2009 global financial crisis. Until 2011, various emerging market economies, especially China and India, pulled the global economy forward, though more as a result of investment-driven labor productivity growth than as a result of total factor productivity (TFP) growth.[2] The past decade's broad-based and stubbornly persistent slowdown has been seen in both labor productivity as well as TFP (Baldwin 2016 , van Ark and Venables 2020 and Van Reenen 2018).

Adding to leadership frustration is the emergence of a new general-purpose technology (GPT). The global cloud computing infrastructure, built by a growing array of providers and the increasing application of artificial intelligence (AI) technology, has produced the "new digital economy" on a platform with massive computing power for a broad set of business, government, and personal digital services. While the adoption of AI, to date, has been limited, the new technology is already providing a rapidly growing collection of services across transportation, health care, information and communication technology (ICT), food, and materials. The technology is beginning to transform services industries just as automation has transformed manufacturing industries (The Economist 2020). The recent extremely rapid development of a series of COVID-19 vaccines—reducing development time from years to months—is, in part, attributable to newly available AI tools and deep learning capabilities (Keshavarzi, Webb, Salem, Cruz, Calad-Thomson, Ghadirian, Collins, Diez-Cecilia, Kelly, Goodarzi, and Yuan 2020).

In an era when data science, software development, and related human capital take on a larger role, intangible capital is embodied in AI and ICT technology (Corrado 2023 forthcoming). If these investments achieve

---

[2] Labor productivity is the inflation-adjusted output of services delivered or goods produced per hour worked. Total factor productivity is the inflation-adjusted output per unit of the weighted average of units of labor, capital, and materials employed. Total factor productivity is an efficiency measure capturing output from the combined inputs employed.

scale, the technology's promise may be realized. Nevertheless, with success measured over decades and an uncertain future, widespread concern for growth prospects remain. The purpose of this book is to explore the social and economic transformation necessary for the global economy to breakthrough from a period of limited growth and increasingly unequally distributed incomes to an era of more robust growth and more equal income distribution.

Changing behavior is never easy. Whether it's the behavior of families, workers, businesses, or governments, change can be painful and resistance is most often very high. In the United States and other developed nations, there is now a substantial legacy of income, wealth, and comfort making the resistance to change powerful. This book will explore the pressures necessary to bring about change and where and when such pressures are likely to be felt. The renewal of the aged capital stock with the new embedded GPT, increased knowledge diffusion and absorptive capacity across the business sector, and shifting labor and capital income shares will all contribute to more rapid growth and more equally distributed income. There is no guarantee that the United States, or any developed nation, will effectively respond to such pressure. It's entirely possible a new era of growth will appear with China and other Asian economies at the center.

The Economic Logic of Long-Term Growth Variation

In 1983, Rosenberg and Frischtak wrote: "No one who has examined the dynamics of capitalist economies over long historical periods can doubt that they experience significant long-term variations in their aggregate performance" (Rosenberg and Frischtak 1983, 146). The interest of Rosenberg and Frischtak was to "examine the economic logic" of such variation and whether such long-term movement is the result of exogenous events in which "the outcome of a summation of random events" drive the observed variation or whether the observed behavior is endogenous. While much of the systemic behavior contributing to long-term variation in aggregate performance has an internal cause—the behavior is endogenous—a meaningful portion of variation develops from external factors—exogenous events. To the extent the 2020–2021 pandemic resulted in behavioral shifts among consumer, workers, and government, such changes are the result of an event whose origins were exogenous to the global economy. Conversely, the response of tangible and intangible capital investment to rising or falling aggregate demand is endogenous to economic, social, or technological causes. The challenge is to parse underlying causes between those that arise from within the system and those responding to external shocks.

Rosenberg and Frischtak were seeking a "coherent explanation" for poor economic performance and propose four requirements that such an explanation must meet—causality, timing, economywide repercussions, and recurrence.[3]

With the benefit of nearly 40 years of scholarship and four decades of data, often produced by turbulent economic performance, Rosenberg's and Frischtak's requirements have been addressed, at least to some degree. Perez (2002) focused on the issue of the timing of industrial revolutions as well as the nonlinear nature of the process in which modest improvement in an early period is followed by a more robust latter stage in which the resolution of high uncertainty results in broad diffusion and adoption. Harberger (1998) was among the first to recognize such staging.[4] Similarly, in the movement between each industrial revolutions' phases, Harberger recognizes complementary inputs as necessary ingredients, for example, physical infrastructure, energy technology, and engineering talent. Likewise, each industrial revolution has been characterized by a newly developed GPT. With a production cost differential, each GPT creates expectations among entrepreneurs that scraping and replacing outdated technology is advantageous, when clarity of a trajectory of future success appears. Finally, the acceptance in the economics literature, over four decades, that technology is embedded in deployed capital ties the

---

[3] Rosenberg and Frischtak cite the work of four scholars—Schumpeter (1939), Freeman (1982), Kondratiev (1979), and Forrester (1981)—each of which they find wanting.

[4] Rostow (1960) postulated growth occurs in five stages of varying length: traditional society, preconditions for takeoff, takeoff, drive to maturity, and age of high mass-consumption. He argued that growth is initially led by a few industrial sectors.

time-consuming process of deploying new tangible capital to the broad availability of the new technology.

Considering the possibility that as each industrial revolution matures stronger growth and more equal incomes result, Rosenberg and Frischtak wrote 40 years ago:

> Interindustry flow of technology is one of the most distinctive characteristics of advanced capitalists societies, where innovations flowing from a few industries may be responsible for generating a vastly disproportionate amount of technological change, productivity improvement and output growth in the economy. (Rosenberg and Frischtak 1983, 150)

While economic historians have focused on industrial revolutions, other economists have provided a detailed development of growth theory.[5] The purpose of this book is to explore the nature and shape of each industrial revolution; define a useful framework for assessing long-term growth for business strategy and public policy; explore how work, business, and government might be transformed; and what conditions or actions will be required to shift the now long-lasting global regime of slow growth to a future of more robust growth and more equal incomes.

What Is Industrial Revolution?

Industrial revolution is the economic and social transformation occurring as a result of the lengthy and complex interaction of capital investment and technological change, along with the redefinition of how work gets done and how businesses are organized. Investment in machinery and equipment can shift from substituting for the skill of workers to complementing the skill of workers and vice versa. Industrial revolution creates the need for (1) new worker skills to build, use, and maintain the new

---

[5] Classical economists, such as Smith (1776), Ricardo (1817), Malthus (1798), and in the mid-20th century Schumpeter (1950), and Swan (1956) provided the basic growth theory ingredients. The work of Solow (1956), Lucas (1988), and Romer (1990) presented the foundation for the work of recent decades.

technology, as well as (2) time to adjust to the new social norms implied by the revolutionary transformation.

Industrial revolution also brings new less expensive energy sources—from water, to steam, to coal, to oil, and to renewables. Each industrial revolution also brings amazing and previously inconceivable technology advances that drive unimagined innovation in businesses, work, and life. Landes describes industrial revolution as a "historical instance of breakthrough" from an existing legacy era to a new era dominated by new technology, new capital investment, and new "forms of industrial organization" (see Landes 1969, 1–2). New business models and new ways of working are as much the essence of industrial revolution as is technology and innovation. Importantly, industrial revolution transforms nations to unequal degrees (see Landes 1969, 1 and 538). Industrial revolution is about shifting the nature of the competition for wealth among nations.

Economists have long-studied industrial revolutions (Kuznets 1955; Kaldor 1961; Kendrick 1961; Denison 1985; Gordon 2016; Crafts 2019). Some focus has been placed on the take-off of industrial activity in the mid-18th century, while other focus has been on periodic technology revolutions and their economic impact (Mokyr 2011). Like much of the developed world, long-run productivity growth in the United Kingdom has followed an unstable path in which growth has been slow to accelerate as a result of industrial revolutions, with peaks in the third quarters of the 19th and 20th centuries (see Crafts 2019 and Broadberry, Campbell, Klein, Overton, and van Leeuwen 2015).

With more than 320 years of UK data covering four industrial revolutions and 100 years of U.S. data covering the better part of two industrial revolutions, some insight can be gleaned (see Table 1.1). With the benefit of scholarship among economic historians and nearly two centuries of hindsight, four industrial revolutions can be examined. There is no expectation that history repeats or that cyclical regularities occur. Rather, the dynamics of growth, innovation, and change, resulting from fundamental economics, which are consistent over extended periods, are of interest. In the words of Rosenberg and Frischtak (1983), this book examines the economic logic of variation in long-term growth.

While understanding the economic logic of long-term growth dynamics principally focuses on developed economies, the experience

Table 1.1 Four industrial revolutions

Era	Industrial Revolution	Years	Technology Innovation
1st	Age of Steam and Railways	1829–1873	"Rocket" Steam Engine (1829)
2nd	Age of Steel, Electricity, and Heavy Engineering	1875–1918	Carnegie Bessemer Steel Plan (1875)
3rd	Age of Oil, Automobiles, and Mass Production	1908–1974	Model-T Mass Production (1908)
4th	Age of Information and Telecommunications	1971 and beyond	Intel Microprocessor Announced (1971)

Source: Perez (2002), p. 78.

of emerging market economies is important as well. Following the 2008–2009 Great Recession and financial crisis, the productivity growth slowdown affected all emerging market regions. However, the slowing was most pronounced in China, East Asia, the Pacific Region, Eastern Europe, Central Asia, and Sub-Saharan Africa. With already weak growth, productivity improvement was limited by slowing capital investment, financial market disruption, and a major commodity price slide. With productivity growth already sluggish prior to the financial crisis, improvement in Latin America, the Caribbean, the Middle East, and North Africa was nonexistent in the crisis' aftermath. Across all the emerging market regions over the period following the crisis, the contribution to productivity growth from human capital was stable while the contribution from capital deepening weakened. With innovation and transformation weak, TFP made a smaller contribution with notable declines in Latin America, the Caribbean, and Sub-Saharan Africa (see Dieppe 2020).

Why do industrial revolutions matter? Beyond the potential creation of income and wealth, industrial revolutions provide a frame of reference for understanding sustained, multidecade periods of faster or slower gross domestic product (GDP) and productivity growth, reducing uncertainty in an unstable environment. Industrial revolutions provide a broad unifying frame to understand the importance of major technological innovations, such as the steam engine, the microprocessor, and the invention of a new method of invention (Moykr 1998). Industrial revolutions have resulted in new general-purpose technologies, have embedded the new technology in tangible and intangible capital, and have driven the innovation of new business processes and business models.

It's easy to get caught up in month-to-month, quarter-to-quarter, and even year-to-year events and developments while losing sight of whether social and economic conditions are improving or worsening over the long term. Some important questions to be answered:

1. Why were the 30 years between 1945 and 1975 a period of rapid growth in real wages, productivity, tangible and intangible capital investment, income, and wealth across the industrialized economies?

2. Conversely, why have the years since 1975 been 45 years of stagnating real wages, slow investment in tangible and intangible capital with limited GDP and productivity growth and labor's income share declining?

3. Despite periods of massive improvement, will the nearly five decades of generally subpar performance give way to a period of renewed robust growth, what will be the nature and extent of the transformation required to realize such gains and which nations will benefit?

4. Why were the 30 years from 1945 to 1975 a period of increasingly more equal income distribution and why have incomes become less equally distributed in recent years?

Positioning economic activity at any point in time appropriately within its industrial revolution provides business leaders with strategic guidance, political leaders with policy direction, and workers with career and job role direction.

Understanding the nature and progress of industrial revolution begins with an understanding of the economic, political, and social forces driving behavior—the logic of long-term growth variation. Each industrial revolution has been accompanied by a new energy technology. The coming revolution will address the climate change and global warming consequences of fossil-fuel technologies and, if successful, over the long-term result in renewable energy sources, reducing energy expense.

However, the transition to a net-zero carbon society in parallel with a transition to advanced, digital, GPT is likely to have substantial implications for productivity. The transition's scale is so large, and replete with a mix of uncertainty and economies of scale in production and discovery, that it cannot be analyzed using a static optimization approach based on historic data (see Geels, Pinkse, and Zenghelis 2021). It is the dynamics of change as experienced in prior industrial revolutions as earlier energy technologies appeared and were deployed at scale that offer insight to the period ahead (see Crafts 2004 and David 1990).

Each revolution proceeds through two periods. The first is the installation period when the next generation of technology is immature and economic activity relies on the capital stock and business practices of the previous era. Second is the deployment period when tangible and intangible capital are renewed, the technology is general-purpose, inexpensive, and ubiquitous, and economic, social, and political institutions are fundamentally transformed. Three phenomena characterize each period: the age of the capital stock, the labor income share, and the rate of knowledge diffusion and thus absorptive capacity (see Table 1.2).

Table 1.2 *Economic logic of industrial revolution*

	Installation Period	**Deployment Period**
Age of Capital Stock	From Previous Era Embodying Old Technology	Renewed Embodying New Technology
Knowledge Diffusion	Limited	Abundant
Labor Income Share	Declining	Increasing to Stable

In the economics literature, consideration of technology has evolved substantially. With the early treatment of Solow (1956), technology was assumed to be exogenous. Thirty years later, Romer (1986) proposed an endogenous treatment with technology responding to income-generating opportunities and delivering increasing returns at the aggregate level. Recent data produced by Kelly, Papanikolaou, Seru, and Taddy (2021) suggest lengthy gestation periods, consistent with the work of both Romer (1986) as well as Perez (2002).

The Dynamics of Industrial Revolution

Industrial revolutions entail the complex dynamics of investment and depreciation. The interrelated dynamics of a broad range of technologies that by their nature are embedded in capital give industrial revolutions a long-life cycle. As is well known, the growth of the capital stock is a function of both the investment in new capital and the depreciation of existing capital. As the capital stock ages and obsolescence increases, tangible and intangible capital becomes less valuable as technology advances. In endogenous growth theory, technological obsolescence drives heterogeneity in cross-sectional profitability and firm-level productivity.[6] At the aggregate level, capital is reallocated and the economy bears the cost of restructuring obsolete technologies, affecting the overall benefit of innovation (Ma 2021).

Technology cycles are also lengthy. Intel was launched in 1971. However, it was not until the mid-1990s when microprocessor technology provided meaningful economic value, as reflected in increased productivity growth (Jorgenson and Stiroh 2000). By 1995, microprocessor innovation resulted in the cost per million computations (CMC) falling by six orders of magnitude over a quarter of a century.[7] An additional 20 years passed, with additional CMC reduction of two further orders of magnitude, before a GPT was available and the global cloud infrastructure was deployed at scale. The realization of a global technology revolution required mobile device innovation as well as a fundamental redesign of the worldwide computing and communication infrastructure across 40 years. To revolutionize economic value, the steam engine required approximately 80 years, while electric power and mass production each required approximately 40 years (Crafts 2004 and David 1990).

Industrial revolutions consist of two periods—an installation period and a deployment period with a major financial crisis intervening.[8] In each period, state dependence plays a role as perceived market and price effects anticipate future income opportunities.

The installation period is a period of experimentation and learning when the new technology finds early, albeit somewhat primitive, applications. While the new technology provides early benefits, innovation in

---

[6] Autor, Dorn, Katz, Patterson, and Van Reenen (2021) point to such heterogeneity as it relates to shifting labor income shares.

[7] Figure 1 in Nordhaus (2021) presents a time trend in the cost per million computations. The data are available www.aeaweb.org/articles?id=10.1257/mac.20170105

[8] In the spirit of Rostow (1960) and Harberger (1998), Perez (2002) proposes each industrial revolution consists of five stages across two periods.

management practices, business models, and new products and services lag. The installation period also carries the legacy of the prior era's long-lived capital, and its embodied technology. With vast wealth having been created in the prior era, the inclination is to defend and grow existing accumulated wealth and resist fundamental transformation (see Gordon 2016 and Mokyr 1998).

Ultimately, the installation period leads to a frenzy of investment in the new technology—for example, the 1990s dot.com bubble and mortgage securitization contribution to the 2008–2009 financial crisis. Financial bubbles arise as investors, eager for returns, overcommit to a new technology that business processes are not yet prepared to exploit at scale (Janeway 2012 and Perez 2002). Value creation is not yet sustainable (see Minsky 1975 and Minsky 1986). On the one hand, existing business models and practices cannot support the fundamental change needed to make the new technology fully effective. On the other hand, the value creation capability of the legacy capital and technology of the prior era begins to fade. The frenzy of new investment fails to persist.

The deployment period is one in which the new technology, along with new business models, social acceptance, and political support are sufficiently in place to deploy, or put in place, the new capital, and its embedded, now general purpose, technology, at a vast scale. Investors now have a deeper understanding of the technology, its rate and pace of diffusion, and the extended time horizon necessary for expected financial return. State dependence is now such that aggregate demand grows at an increased pace and factor demand grows in a complementary fashion.

Schumpeter (1950) coined the term "creative destruction," which is the continuous process of product and service creation, business process improvement, and business model innovation. Through creative destruction new, innovative capabilities replace existing processes that are rendered obsolete over time. The restructuring process runs through major aspects of macroeconomic performance, not only long-run growth but also economic fluctuations, structural adjustment, and the functioning of factor markets. Over the long run, Caballero (2010) estimates the process of creative destruction accounts for over 50 percent of productivity growth.

The intersection of technological innovation and creative destruction is at the heart of the distinction between the installation period and the deployment period. The installation period is one in which technological innovation rises in importance as the period progresses. Creative destruction births new firms and new jobs—social media, search, e-commerce, with jobs such as data science, with gains principally among productivity leaders. In the deployment period, creative destruction, or process transformation, becomes more widespread and intense as the now, inexpensive, GPT is available to change how businesses, households, and governments function and operate while also creating new jobs and new tasks in the context of existing jobs. The nature of creative destruction differs in the installation and deployment periods.

Harberger (1998), in his American Economic Association Presidential Address, anticipated the work of Perez, capturing the essence of the installation period and deployment period distinction. He highlights two types of growth. One, with focused creative destruction is characterized as "mushroom" growth with "real cost reduction stemming from 1001 different causes" with a limited number of sectors, industries, or firms experiencing much-improved productivity, as is seen in the installation period. The second type of growth is what Harberger calls "yeasty" growth "with very broad and general externalities, like externalities linked to the growth of the total stock of knowledge or of human capital, or bought about by economies of scale tied to the scale of the economy as a whole." Once productivity improvement spreads widely across the economy, "yeasty" growth, as is seen in the deployment period, responds to the adoption of a GPT with substantial creative destruction and business process transformation (see van Ark, de Vries, and Erumban 2020).

With strong TFP growth over the 1948–1975 period and an initially aged capital stock from the earlier era, the deployment of the then-mature Third Industrial Revolution's mass production technology resulted in strong growth in investment spending. Conversely, in the 1975–2010 installation period of the Fourth Industrial Revolution, the young capital stock at the beginning of the period, the emergence of the new electronics and information technology (IT) with only very limited initial absorption in business processes, and slow TFP growth, collectively slowed investment spending from the strong growth of the pre-1975 period.

Absorptive capacity is the ability of a firm to recognize the value of new, innovative, external information; assimilate such information; and create economic value. Innovative capabilities are, theoretically, a function of prior related knowledge and diversity, making absorptive capacity path dependent with investment in tangible and intangible capital necessary for future success (see Cohen and Levinthal 1990). Knowledge diffusion is required for knowledge absorption. A decrease in knowledge diffusion from productivity leaders to laggard firms, suggests a decrease in aggregate supply, and all else equal, implies increased markups and profits, a labor share decrease, and a shift to more concentrated sectors where more productive firms pay more to their workers (see Akcigit and Ates 2021).

Empirically, a decline in knowledge diffusion is observed between productivity leaders and laggard firms in the 1980–2010 period—approximately the most recent installation period, with new business formation declining. Conversely, recently assembled data—see Figure 4.2—show a substantial increase in new business formation in the 1948–1980 period—the 3rd Industrial Revolution's deployment period, suggesting that, perhaps, knowledge diffusion and new business formation could both show an increase in the period ahead.

Declining labor income share accompanying eroding business formation across the industrialized economies since 1980 is, by now, an established fact. However, causality is very much an unsettled issue. Recent work by Autor, Dorn, Katz, Patterson, and Van Reenen (2020) suggests a steep increase in sales concentration among firms with faster productivity growth. These productivity leaders realize higher markups, enhanced innovation. These leaders are each industry superstars with new technology rapidly emerging at scale and labor costs as a percent of revenue are lower-than-expected.[9] Consequently, the superstars make an important contribution to declines in labor income share.

High-productivity firms with leading-edge capabilities are able to capture the early benefits of the industrial revolution's new technology. Lagging firms wait until the new technology is less expensive, well understood, and the extent and nature of the necessary creative destruction is clear. When knowledge diffusion and absorptive capacity become widespread, a broader cross-section of industry firms are able to adopt the new technology, creatively destruct their existing business models and

---

[9] Autor et al. (2020) label the productivity leaders as superstars. While it is common to think such firms as Facebook, Google, Amazon, and so on as superstars, in fact, these leaders are found across all industries.

processes, innovate with lessons learned from industry leaders, and profitably invest in new tangible and intangible capital. With such widespread adoption, macroeconomic benefits are likely with more rapid output and productivity growth and low inflation.[10]

However, after passing through the financial crisis and correcting asset values, if the deployment period is to become a reality, sufficient social, economic, and political pressure must be present to cause workers, households, businesses, and governments to fundamentally change behavior (see Posen 2021). Growth in the prior installation period created conflict. Creative destruction is necessary to destroy the monopoly rents that accumulated. The more rapid growth and improved productivity performance in the anticipated deployment period requires a new economic and social regime.

Three Forces of Industrial Revolution

Chapter 2 defines the emergence of industrial revolutions at the intersection of tangible and intangible capital investment, new technology, and the creative destruction driving business model and business process transformation and delivering productivity growth.

The chapter presents an empirical overview, providing the context for the economics of industrial revolutions. Recent advances in natural language processing have allowed Kelly, Papanikolaou, Seru, and Taddy (2021) to provide detailed measurement of technology deployment. Surges in technology deployment and follow-on major financial crises are introduced as an element of each era's transformation. Together, the alignment allows for detailed dating of each industrial era. The chapter examines the embedded nature of technology in tangible and intangible capital. Recent eras, where data are readily available, are characterized by (1) the nature of capital investment and the aging of the capital stock, (2) the extent of knowledge diffusion and absorptive capacity, and (3) shifting labor and capital income share.

---

[10] As Autor et al. (2020) show shifting income shares, growing from firm-level productivity differentials, in the Fourth Industrial Revolution's installation period. Allen (2009) shows similar income shifts in the First Industrial Revolution.

Chapter 3 tells the story of four industrial revolutions, as economic historians have recorded them. Historians have highlighted several elements that have had enduring importance across each industrial revolution. Advances in technology and massive tangible capital investment requirements are the foundation of each industrial revolution. The role of falling prices, the appearance of rapidly increasing demand, the need for scale, the benefit of business model innovation, and the opportunity for new energy sources are all elements witnessed repeatedly. Importantly, human resources are critical. Success depends on the available talent and skill. Finally, what also matters is the dynamics of change as the technology matures, capital investment accumulates, and demand is satisfied. The success of each industrial revolution is ultimately about the pressures and dislocation necessary to force migration from one era to another.

Chapter 4, which provides a more technical discussion than other chapters, begins with an exploration of knowledge diffusion and absorptive capacity across the periods of each industrial revolution. In the installation period, knowledge diffusion is limited as firms at technology's leading edge attract the necessary skill, engage in innovative activity, and achieve early success. With innovation proceeding rapidly and new previously unheard-of products and services appearing, trade secrets, and patents are enforced while firms not at the leading edge lack the necessary skill to join the frenzy. The successful innovators become industry superstars with new technology rapidly appearing. As the technology matures, business models transform, and a new regime emerges, the deployment period brings much greater knowledge diffusion and deeper absorptive capacity across a much wider universe of firms. With stronger economic and productivity growth, labor demand strengthens and labor's share of income begins to climb.

The existence of productivity leaders suggests there are productivity laggards, creating persistent productivity differences, even at the subindustry level. The laggards lack the management skill, technology, talent, and the IT investments necessary to migrate to the productivity frontier. With the technology maturing, the deployment period is the opportunity for the laggards to narrow the gap with gains that boost aggregate productivity and income. In recent years, the laggards have been catching up, but at a slower pace particularly in industries using digital technologies, digital skills, and more intense general skills.

While more productive workers, whether they are in superstar firms or lagging firms, are typically rewarded with higher wages and compensation, workers who are more fully engaged, in part as a result of more competitive compensation, are also more productive. There is a positive feedback loop, creating a virtuous cycle. Worker engagement is a result of workers' skills, satisfaction, career paths, and compensation while more engaged workers are more productive and, thus, better compensated and supported in their careers.

As services sectors have become a larger part of the global economy, the interest and ability of workers to fully engage has become an important driver of productivity and profitability. Services, by their nature, are provided by skilled, competent workers. There is a growing body of economics literature that seemingly confirms causality. With global services sectors continuing in importance in the period ahead, worker engagement will take on added significance as the productivity laggards absorb the newly available technology and business models. Creative destruction and transformation will be widespread.

Finally, Chapter 4 addresses the much-debated topic of the future of work. With worker engagement an important contributor to productivity, whether technology capital automates or augments worker effort matters. Viewed through the lens of industrial revolution, installation periods, for example 1975 through 2008, have been periods in which capital has often—but not always—substituted for labor. Conversely, deployment periods, for example 1945 to 1975, have been years in which labor and capital are complementary. During deployment periods, with robust and growing aggregate demand, labor is in high demand and wage rate increases accelerate. Workers find they have leverage. But, all jobs change. While occupations tend to change slowly, new tasks are created and new skills are required. More jobs are created than disappear.

Building on the dynamics of change outlined in Chapter 4, Chapter 5 examines three sets of growth resources—advanced digital technology, tangible and intangible capital investment, and labor quality. Economists focus on the needed resources on the right side of the production function. The benefits of the deployment period will be realized only in response to widespread resource reprioritization. The dynamics of change and transformation are explored in this chapter.

Much current empirical research finds AI applications in early deployment. Zolas, Kroff, Brynjolfsson, McElheran, Beede, Buffington, Goldschlag, Foster, and Dinlersoz (2020) provide possibly the most extensive estimate of AI technology usage. They found in 2017, across AI-related technologies, for all firms in the United States the aggregate adoption rate was 6.6 percent.[11] Zolas et al. also find adoption was skewed. While the heaviest concentration was among a small subset of older and larger firms, an increasing number of new, young, born-on-the-web, still quite small firms are also adopters. Cloud services adoption displayed modest adoption in 2017, with a large share of firms hosting at least one IT function in the cloud. But cloud usage was significantly lower than the adoption rates of digital business information, which is nearly universal.

Chapter 5 also explores response of tangible capital investment to changes in the cost of capital, adoption of new technology, and the availability of intangible assets—workers skills, organization capital, and innovation. Crouzet and Eberly (2020) have done the most extensive recent work. They find that tangible capital investment has responded to (1) earned excess profit—rents earned by tangible capital, (2) the value of intangible capital, and (3) the interaction between the two. However, when Crouzet and Eberly expand the definition of intangibles to include research, development, organizational capital, innovation, and transformation, the combined contribution of growth in the intangible capital stock and rents generated by intangible capital increases to about two-thirds. Crouzet's and Eberly's work suggests that the growth of investment has become much more dependent on the availability of a skilled workforce and somewhat less dependent on the cost of physical capital. Similarly, the notion of secular stagnation, as formulated by Summers (2014) with a focus on real interest rates, is further suggestive of the diminishing role of the cost of capital incenting investment spending growth.

---

[11] Unpublished estimates provided by a global technology provider found 4 percent of global large enterprises were operating AI solutions in 2016, 5 percent were operating such solutions in 2018, and 9 percent in 2020.

Chapter 5 concludes with a focus on worker engagement. The assertation is that the social and economic benefits of the Fourth Industrial Revolution will—in important part—be a function of the skill and engagement of workers. The 1945–1975 deployment period of the Third Industrial Revolution was characterized by massive fiscal infrastructure investment to rebuild war-torn nations; create military and space program intellectual property investments in the context of United States, Western Europe, and Soviet strategic competition; and launch new institutional arrangements, such as the Treaty of Detroit that settled employer–employee relationships for years. With the importance of human resources—intangible assets—in facilitating the deployment of new technology embedded in tangible capital and with the adoption of AI applications redefining how work gets done, the compensation, skill development, satisfaction, career development, and engagement of workers will take on elevated importance in the period ahead. As recently summarized by Jorgenson, Ho, and Samuels (2019), labor quality has long been a known determinant of productivity. More recently, worker engagement has taken on increased importance in supporting improved productivity.

Is a Growth Revolution Ahead?

Chapter 6 concludes with possible outcomes. Major economic shocks, such as the 2020–2021 global pandemic, can result in hysteresis effects and disappointing outcomes. If a new era fails to emerge, such disappointing outcomes could include a prolonged period of stagflation as the recent experience with more rapid inflation persists with slow growth. Conversely, if economic, social, and political disruption is severe enough, creative destruction, accompanied by social, political, and economic transformation, can ensue resulting in robust growth, increased tangible and intangible capital investment, and improved productivity.

The current pandemic, at least for 2020 through 2021, has resulted in reduced labor force participation, increased depression, and elevated anxiety, and increased personal savings. The psychological effects of the current pandemics are not new, and the resulting economic outcomes have been consistent over centuries. Perhaps surprisingly, with 700 years of UK data, recent scholarship has found across 19 previous pandemics over the last millennium, postpandemic periods have brought depressed real interest rates, rising real wages, and stronger real GDP per capita growth. Tangible and intangible capital are destroyed in wars but not in pandemics. Instead, pandemics appear to induce labor scarcity and a shift to precautionary savings—much as today.

Economic shocks—financial crises, pandemics, and wars—have played an important role in each industrial revolution. In an economic environment in which stability is highly variable achieving balance between those business leaders, workers, and elected public officials who seek to follow and maintain a traditional approach and those whose learning and adjustments costs are suitable for nontraditional approaches is important, but achieving a balanced equilibrium is critical. The culture that defines traditional business and work arrangements matter but transitioning to new business models, new ways of working, and new political engagement is necessary for improved economic and productivity growth and more equal income distribution. Business leaders—especially those with lagging productivity growth—will need to adopt the new technology, engage in creative destruction, and invest in tangible and intangible capital. Workers, who are reluctant to experience disruption and transformation in their work arrangements will need the necessary support and incentives to embrace change.

Over recent decades, a wide array of fiscal, tax, and monetary policies have been deployed to support growth, but unsatisfactory outcomes remain. While finding the best and most effective government policy and programs configurations is important, it seems unlikely there is a silver bullet yet to be found. More likely, a new social contract is required in which workers, business leaders, and elected public officials can come to together, as a result of the pressure and dislocation from unsatisfactory economic outcomes and the 2020–2021 pandemic. It will be in their individual and collective interest to transform economic activity, work, and governance to realize the benefits of a period of more robust growth and a more equal distribution of incomes.

Finally, Chapter 6 proposes a Growth and Fairness Agenda through which stronger economic and productivity growth can be possible.

Recognize Traditional Policy Actions May Be Insufficient to Achieve Stronger Long-Term Growth

Despite taking a wide range of fiscal, tax, and monetary policy actions, economic and productivity growth remains disappointing. There is no silver bullet. More importantly, the recent challenge of faltering democratic processes, and the possibility of increased autocratic rule, across the developed nations has raised concerns that are likely to be a more serious impediment to growth than is inconsistent or ineffective fiscal, tax, or monetary policy. The inability of political leaders to take actions in the general interest of their constituents is sufficient to prevent policy-led improvements in economic and productivity growth. Consistent leadership matters. Independent of the ruling party, confidence among small and medium business leaders matters as the technology evolves. Investment in the talent and engagement of workers, which is made by both workers and business leaders—will require considerable capital reallocation from alternative uses and, thus, confidence among both workers and business leaders.

Promote Improved Confidence and a Positive Outlook Among Small and Medium Enterprises (SMEs)

If income and productivity growth is to improve, economic activity must be reallocated to the most efficient firms and productivity lagging firms must be willing to invest in the necessary skill, technology, and change management. For SMEs, size often acts as a barrier to adoption and, as such, smaller businesses continue to lag in digital transformation. Further AI technology innovation is required to reduce cost, increase ease of use, expand the pace of adoption, and open the opportunity for broad SME adoption. To address such gaps, SMEs can source external AI expertise and solutions. Software as a Service (SaaS) and Machine Learning as a Service (MLaaS) offer advantages such as scalability, cost, technical knowledge, and embedded digital security. However, understanding AI benefits and building an effective transformation is required. Reskilling SME business leaders and workers to ensure work processes redesign and AI models training is critical. Broad social recognition of the important role SMEs play, increased policy consistency, reasonable tax and regulatory policy, and continued AI technology advancement will all support productivity gains among current lagging firms.

Encourage Advances in AI Technology While Addressing Risks and Fairness Issues

As we will show, AI solutions have been adopted by only approximately 10 percent of potential applications. With much concern over job losses associated with the deployment of AI, the technology remains in much too limited deployment to account for job losses that have already occurred. We can't blame AI technology for more than a small percentage of job losses. As the technology becomes less expensive and easier to use, more jobs could be created than are lost for a net gain. Depending on the competitive environment and the extent of creative destruction, AI innovation can result in more robust growth. As with any new technology that could reshape the future, there are risks and ethical pitfalls that could arise. If AI technology is to be successful, all risks must be taken seriously. However, the risk that has received the most attention is fairness. With limited data, bias is easily inadvertently encoded in AI models. While the benefit of AI technology seems likely to be realized, there is much to be done to address job losses, solution prioritization, business risks, and fairness.

Support Deeper Worker Engagement Between Business Leaders and Workers

We will make the case that, not only worker skills, but also worker engagement matters. Workers who feel they are treated fairly in terms of compensation, career advancement, education, and training report high levels of job satisfaction and are more productive. The recent postpandemic wave of worker resignations suggests workers are taking it upon themselves to find opportunities that could result in improved engagement and follow-on productivity gains. Government education and training programs can help, even starting as soon as early childhood. In addition, many business leaders have recognized that workers in the millennial and

Gen-X cohort expect greater fulfillment and satisfaction from their work experience and have adjusted work arrangements accordingly. While the future is uncertain, it's possible that a generational shift in attitudes about work and careers will create sufficient pressure to fundamentally alter employer–employee relationships. Finally, all jobs will change. New technology will continue to automate tasks that many workers currently perform. However, the creation of new tasks and increased labor demand resulting from more robust growth will provide meaningful job opportunities for a slowly growing workforce.

Seek a New Social Contract Among an Ecosystem of Workers, Businesses, and Governments

Improved economic performance is only likely to be realized when workers, business leaders, and elected public officials have a view of a common interest and an ability to comprise. A new social contract will permit the necessary working relationships that will support growth and more vigorous income expansion. SMEs, because they lack large enterprise resources, have a broad range of unmet needs, and can realize substantial benefit from a robust ecosystem of partners. Their limited size creates a need for capabilities and resources that would make them more productive, including talented workers, technology, finance, and managerial practices. Early-stage innovative start-ups, established successful start-ups, growing medium-size companies, and struggling medium-size companies are the SMEs that are most likely to benefit from ecosystem support. Limited familiarity with AI, expensive talent, and constrained investment capital can slow AI adoption by SMEs. However, some governments have begun digital-productivity adoption programs to help SMEs deploy AI technologies in their processes and products. These programs often depend on an ecosystem of different players and professionals.

CHAPTER 2

Industrial Revolution, Growth, and Technological Change

In this chapter, (1) growth is examined in the context of long-term stability and instability that has been observed over 250 years, (2) surges and plunges of innovative activity are identified as are the coincident follow-on of major global financial crises, and (3) four industrial revolutions are defined and important characteristics of each are observed in the volatility of nonresidential tangible and intangible capital, labor productivity, and GDP.

The focus of economists in the post-World War II era on growth, capital investment, and productivity received its most significant boost from the work of Solow (1956). While others had pointed to a long-time horizon as a topic of interest, it was Solow's 1956 work that created the original framework characterizing the economy's long-run growth path as well as the conditions necessary for an optimal outcome.

In parallel with Solow's work, Schumpeter (1950) expanded the focus beyond the appearance of new technology to the process of creative destruction in which

> ... new innovations continually emerge and render existing technologies obsolete, new firms continually arrive to compete with existing firms, and new jobs and activities arise and replace existing jobs and activities. (See Aghion, Antonin, and Bunel 2021, 1)

While Solow's approach provided the key to systematic growth accounting developed by Zvi Griliches, Edward Denison, Dale Jorgenson, and Angus Maddison, Solow had much less to say about technology and innovation. While Schumpeter and other classical economists didn't completely address technology, they did focus on growth dynamics.

It wasn't until the work of Paul Romer that neoclassical economists took technology seriously. And it took years before Philippe Aghion, Daron Acemoglu, David Autor, and others made important contributions to understanding technology. In the meantime, the evolutionary economists, such as Richard Nelson, Sidney Winter, Brian Arthur, and Carlota Perez carried the torch, which is why it is appropriate to combine modern growth economics and evolutionary economics going forward.

Similarly, alternative approaches to technology and growth, such as those offered by Nikolai Kondratieff, Joseph Schumpeter, Simon Kuznets, and more recently Jay Forrester, have generally failed to provide sustained and persistent insight. In contrast to the notion of repeated regularities, Maddisson argues each era is different and should be considered on its own merits. Maddisson concludes:

> The existence of regular long-term rhythmic movements in economic activity is not proven, ... Nevertheless, it is clear that major changes in growth momentum have occurred since 1820, and some explanation is needed. In my view it can be sought not in systematic long waves, but in specific disturbances of an ad hoc character. Major system shocks change the momentum of capitalist development at certain points. Sometimes they are more or less accidental in origin; sometimes they occur because some inherently unstable situation can no longer be lived with but has finally broken down (e.g., the Bretton Woods fixed exchange rate system). (See Maddisson 1982)

Maddison recognized that while random events can influence outcomes, endogenous behavior is also at work. Maddison defined four periods of growth across the developed world between 1870 and 1973 (see Maddison 1979, 1982, 1991).

By the mid-1980s, three decades after Solow's pathbreaking work, with technology-related innovation beginning to take off, Romer (1990) provided the necessary add-ons with a set of knowledge-creating drivers.[1] While Solow assumed an exogenous steady-state path for technology, Romer focused on the development of new technologies in market economies through profit-maximizing research and development. However, Romer's model of innovation-led growth did not include creative destruction (see Aghion, Antonin, and Bunel 2021).

First, Romer introduced a new view of technology. While Romer recognized that individual firms are subject to diminishing returns, at higher aggregate levels—industry, city, nation—increasing returns are realized as technology is deployed across geographic and political entities. Romer's insight was that the capital stock consists of both tangible and intangible assets. The focus was on how market economies develop new technologies, endogenously, as profit-maximizing research and development responds to perceived opportunities.

Intangible assets grow out of ideas that Romer famously defined as having properties as nonrivalrous—easily shared—and nonexcludable—cannot be owned.[2] Many ideas have such properties and, as ideas spread, innovation abounds, intangible assets expand, and growth quickens, especially among the most advanced economies. [3, 4]

Second, by the mid-1980s, Romer had the benefit of the Penn World data, a comprehensive cross-country data set, (Summers and Heston 1984) and the Maddison data for countries in the 18th, 19th, and early 20th centuries (Bolt and Van Zanden 2020). Romer showed that productivity growth across the three leading economies of the 18th and

---

[1] See Royal Swedish Academy of Science (2018) for a summary of the Solow and Romer work.

[2] Romer cites, as a contrary illustration, encoded satellite television broadcasts, a rivalrous, excludable good, that is intellectual property. Pure public goods are both nonrival and nonexcludable.

[3] Haskel and Westlake (2018) argue that intangible capital is largely nonexcludable.

[4] Concurrent with Romer's early work, Lucas (1988) developed a theory of human capital as the driver of growth, along with tangible capital. The endogenous buildup of intangible capital, augmenting labor input in Solow's model, prevents the returns from capital from falling, allowing continued accumulation of tangible capital as well (see Royal Swedish Academy of Sciences 2018).

19th centuries—Netherlands, United Kingdom, and United States—increased monotonically (Romer 1986,1009). Further Romer observed:

> These rates also suggest a positive rather than a negative trend, but measuring growth rates over 40-year intervals hides a substantial amount of year-to-year or even decade-to-decade variation in the rate of growth. (Romer 1986, 1009)

Long-Term Growth and Economic Instability

At the heart of Romer's work was a focus on (1) an endogenous response to income-generating opportunities producing increasing returns to scale in technology deployment, (2) diminishing returns at the firm level, and (3) decade-to-decade variation in national growth rates.[5] (See Romer 1987a, 1987b, 1990 and 1991.) With the advantage of nearly 40 years of additional data, a global financial crisis, and the Maddison project data, Figure 2.1 shows U.S. and UK GDP growth. Over the nearly 200 years, growth varied across the decades in both economies with U.S. growth trending down late in the 20th century and early in the 21st century.[6]

Despite Romer's insight, the economics literature has struggled to identify causal factors influencing growth and the policies affecting growth (Banerjee and Duflo 2019, 180). Indeed Easterly (2001), a noted skeptic of growth theory, asserts national growth rates change significantly from decade to decade with limited sustained impact.[7] A significant impediment in understanding growth, especially in advanced economies, has

---

[5] For a discussion of Romer's views of increasing returns to scale at the aggregate level and diminishing returns at the firm level, see Banerjee and Duflo (2019), pp. 162–165. For Easterly's view, see Banerjee and Duflo (2019), p. 181.

[6] For the Hodrick-Prescott (HP) filter see Hodrick and Prescott (1997). Hamilton (2017) presents evidence against using the HP filter, citing spurious dynamic relations. Hodrick (2020) finds the HP filter is better than the Hamilton alternative at extracting the cyclical component of several simulated time series calibrated to approximate U.S. real GDP.

[7] Easterly's critique is principally focused on the failure to understand the drivers of growth in less-developed and emerging market economies. While he is explicit that he does not take on a general survey of growth, his broader observation is, implicitly, the gap in understanding the determinants of growth.

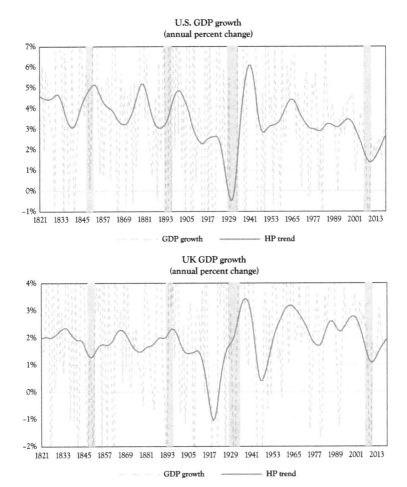

Figure 2.1 U.S. and UK GDP growth

Source: Maddison Project Database (MPD) 2020 with author's calculations. Major Financial Crises from Perez (2002).

been the difficulty in measuring the technological progress that so concerned Solow and Romer.

To fill the measurement gap, recent work by Kelly, Papanikolaou, Seru, and Taddy (2021) apply natural language processing (NLP) methods to data from U.S. patent documents to build indices of breakthrough innovations. Kelly et al. define breakthrough innovations as distinct improvements in the technological frontier that become the foundation on which subsequent innovations are built.

Kelly et al. develop "measures of textual similarity to quantify commonality in the topical content of each pair of patents." They identify significant, high-quality patents as those whose content is novel and impactful on future patents. As a "ground truth" data set, Kelly et al. identify major technological breakthroughs across the 19th and 20th centuries. These breakthroughs include watershed inventions such as the telegraph, the elevator, the typewriter, the telephone, electric light, the airplane, frozen foods, television, plastics, electronics, computers, and advances in modern genetics (see Gordon 2016 for a detailed discussion).

The measures of patent significance, developed with the NLP patent citation method, perform substantially better than citation counts in identifying the "ground truth" of major technological breakthroughs (see Figure 2.2). Validation shows the relationship of the measures to market value. With novel contributions adopted by subsequent technologies, the measures are capturing the scientific value of a patent (see also Bloom, Hassan, Kalyani, Lerner, and Tahoun 2021).

The resulting Kelly et al. aggregate innovation index shows three technology surges—mid- to late-19th century, the 1920s and 1930s, and the post-1980 period. Advances in electricity and transportation in the 1880s; agriculture in the 1900s; chemicals and electricity in the 1920s and 1930s; and computers and communication in the post-1960s all contribute to high-value innovation (see Figure 2.2).

The Kelly et al. innovation index is also a strong predictor of aggregate TFP for which a one-standard deviation increase in the index is associated with a 0.5 to 2 percentage point higher annual productivity growth over the subsequent 5 to 10 years. By mapping technology to industries, sectoral technological breakthrough indexes span the entire sample. Sectors that have breakthrough innovations experience faster growth in productivity than sectors that do not.

These breakthrough innovations are of the nature of the advances that Romer had in mind when suggesting that many such ideas, because they are protected by patents or as trade secrets, are nonrival and nonexcludable. Indeed, the Kelly et al. innovation index in Figure 2.2 shows periodic surges of very significant ideas have spread repeatedly, widely, and rapidly over nearly two centuries, suggesting the presence of increasing returns to scale at the industry and national levels.

The periodic technology surges, as identified by Kelly et al., are further characterized by Perez (2002). The revolutionary technology that drives the surges creates investment in new industries, most often by new,

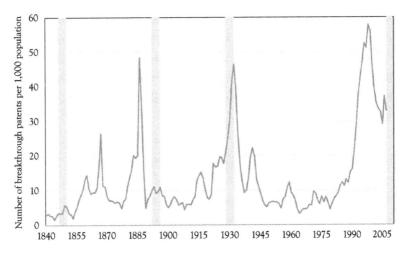

Figure 2.2 Breakthrough patents (top 5 percent significant patents per capita)

Source: Kelly et al. (2020). (Kelly et al. Figure 4, Panel A shows Top 10 percent significant patents per capital. Additional data are available from online data.) Gray bars are major financial crises.

young entrepreneurs, Perez suggests. Funding of such ventures reallocates capital and creates new sources of wealth. New infrastructure is created and existing industries are modernized. The clustering of technological innovation is a further illustration that a broad class of ideas are nonrivalrous and nonexcludable, generating increasing returns to scale.

Perez describes periodic technology revolutions and associated creative destruction as:

> Strongly interrelated constellation of technical innovations, generally including an important all-persuasive low-cost input, often a source of energy, sometimes a crucial material, plus significant new products and processes and a new infrastructure. The latter usually changes the frontier in speed and reliability of transportation and communications, while drastically reducing their cost. (Perez 2002, 8)

Innovation, Financial Crises, and Growth

Periodic technology and innovation surges have been frequently followed by major financial crises. Among the most well-known are the events of the 20th and early 21st century—the Great Depression of the 1930s and the Great Recession and Global Financial Crisis of 2007 to 2009. Scholars, who have carefully tracked such events, agree that both downturns qualify as major financial crises. Aliber and Kindleberger (2015), Reinhart and Rogoff (2009), and Perez (2002), all identify the Great Depression and the Global Financial Crisis as financial crises that are among the historically largest.[8]

Building on the work of Minsky (1975) and Minsky (1986), Aliber and Kindleberger identify crises that follow an exogenous shock that sets off a mania. The mania involves a specific object of speculation, such as commodities, real estate, bonds, and equities as well as a source of monetary expansion. Perez builds on the work of Minsky, Aliber, and Kindleberger.

Reinhart and Rogoff (2009), famously, develop a quantitative history of financial crisis. Between 1800 and 2009, Reinhart and Rogoff identify 250 external sovereign debt default episodes, 68 domestic debt defaults, and 270 banking crises. Reinhart and Rogoff also highlight inflation and currency crises. However, they label four episodes as global financial crises. Reinhart and Rogoff define global financial crises as having four main elements: (1) a global financial center is involved in a systemic crisis, (2) two or more global regions are involved, (3) the number of countries involved in each region is three or more, and (4) the Reinhart and Rogoff composite GDP-weighted average global financial turbulence index is at least one standard deviation above average.[9] In Reinhart and Rogoff's view, such financial crises share three characteristics—a deep and prolonged asset market crash, a banking crisis that is followed by profound declines in output and employment, and a vast expansion in the value of government debt.

As measured by Reinhart and Rogoff, financial crises bring declines in real housing prices averaging 35 percent, a three-and-a-half-year equity price decline averaging 56 percent, peak to trough output declines averaging 9 percent, and an increase in the value of government debt rising to 86 percent of GDP in the major post-World War II episodes.

---

[8] Aliber and Kindleberger (2015) is the seventh edition of the Kindleberger's classic treatment of the history of financial crises, first published in 1978. Aliber joined Kindleberger after the publication of the fourth edition in 2000.

[9] See Reinhart and Rogoff. 2009. Box 16.1, pp. 260–261.

Table 2.1 summarizes each of the four revolutions of the industrial era. Perez (2002) asserts that, initially, the technology is "installed" with an early irruption in which new products and industries experience explosive growth and rapid innovation. However, the technology remains nascent and new applications are limited. Over time the power of the new technology becomes apparent, with applications appearing at an increasing rate. Continuing innovation drives down the cost of the new technology, setting the stage for deployment at scale.

However, soon a frenzy appears. While great wealth is created, as seen recently in social media and search, the broad cross-section of business models and societal institutions remain tied to the prior era. The rush of funding into new ventures results in overinvestment and an inability to fully transform household and industrial uses and fully exploit the new technology. To prepare for the period of growth ahead, the ensuing financial crisis is needed to cleanse balance sheets, alter family and household practices, and force complete creative destruction and the transformation of business processes.

The financial crisis provides the preparation for the "deployment" period. The broad economic contraction causes businesses and households to search for new more efficient processes and practices. The new technology finds new synergy. Business and government practices are transformed and societal norms experience very significant change. Investors begin to understand both the potential opportunities that may soon appear with the needed capital investment and new technology as well as the extended time horizon for financial return. Financial capital becomes a growth influence as investors are able to guide business transformation to effectively exploit the new technology (Janeway 2012; Perez 2002).

Gordon (2016) provides a rich and masterful overview of the social and economic transformation that reshaped the United States during the Second and Third Industrial Revolutions, aligned with Perez (2002). Similarly, Mokyr (1998) details the social and economic transformation of the 1870–1914 Second Industrial Revolution, aligned with Perez. As new technologies were deployed, social and economic activity transitioned from the installation period through a financial crisis into the deployment period. Gordon provides a detailed description of how technology, growth, and institutional change interacted to transform social

Table 2.1 *Industrial revolution dates and eras*

Era	Industrial Revolution	Years	Technology Innovation	Installation		Major Financial Crisis	Deployment	
				Irruption	Frenzy		Synergy	Maturity
1st	Age of Steam and Railways	1829–1873	"Rocket" Steam Engine (1829)	1830s	1840s	1848–1850	1850–1857	1857–1873
2nd	Age of Steel, Electricity and Heavy Engineering	1875–1918	Carnegie Bessemer Steel Plan (1875)	1875–1884	1884–1893	1893–1895	1895–1907	1908–1918*
3rd	Age of Oil, Automobiles and Mass Production	1908–1974	Model-T Mass Production (1908)	1908–1920*	1920–1929	Europe 1929–1933 U.S. 1929–1943	1943–1959	1960–1974*
4th	Age of Information and Tele-communications	1971–2019	Intel Microprocessor Announced (1971)	1971–1987*	1987–2007	2007–2010	2010	

Source: Perez (2002), p. 78.

*Phase overlaps between successive surges

and economic activity and provide meaningful improvements in living standards, health, and personal comfort. During such periods, economic growth and productivity begin to quicken, the economy and society enter a "golden era." Finally, as the new technology and the transformation resulting in the creative destruction matures, rapid growth continues over time. Technology and transformation opportunities become fully exploited. Market saturation creates limits to further growth. Increasing rates of inflation begin to appear.

Table 2.2 provides a view of growth across the eras. The last column shows the successively slower growth rates across the eras as the U.S. economy has matured. The 19th-century eras benefited from continued growth, even during major financial crises and relatively stronger growth in the synergy phase. Conversely, in the 20th century and the early 21st century, financial crises brought significant activity declines while the synergy phases have brought relatively weak growth. The severe financial crises and the weaker expansions in the recent period is suggestive of the transformation challenges delaying the appearance of new opportunities. The weak 1.5 percent annual growth in the 2010–2019 period is symptomatic of the delay in deploying the current revolution's technology.[10]

Crafts (2021a) shows, during Britain's First Industrial Revolution, output growth increased only marginally. However, capital deepening, human capital, and TFP growth were sources of growth. As expected, larger increases occurred in the deployment period. The experience of the First Industrial Revolution is seen by Crafts as an exception to revolutions that followed. The essence of the First Industrial Revolution was not rapid productivity growth in the short run but the "invention of a new method of invention," which increased technological progress in the long run.

Table 2.3 provides a view of tangible and intangible capital investment. As shown across the table's bottom row, capital deepening increases more rapidly during the Third Industrial Revolution deployment period during which the stock of capital grew at a 2.0 percent annual rate. Growth slowed in the Fourth Industrial Revolution to 1.2 percent annual rate during the installation period. While the technology irrupts

---

[10] Chapter 5 will discuss the delay in detail.

Table 2.2 *U.S. GDP growth by industrial revolution*

Era	Industrial Revolution	Years	U.S. GDP Growth (Average Annual Growth Rates Major Financial Crises Peak to Trough Change)					
			Irruption	Frenzy	Major Financial Crisis	Synergy	Maturity	Total
1st	Age of Steam and Railways	1829–1873	5.0%	3.4%	+3.3%	5.2%	3.8%	4.2%
2nd	Age of Steel, Electricity and Heavy Engineering	1875–1918	5.1%	2.7%	+8.8%	4.3%	3.2%	3.7%
3rd	Age of Oil, Automobiles, and Mass Production	1908–1974	2.6%	3.4%	-30.5%	2.3%	4.0%	3.0%
4th	Age of Information and Telecommunications	1971–2019	3.2%	3.1%	-3.1%	1.5%	—	2.8%
Average			4.0%	3.1%	-5.4%	3.3%	3.7%	3.3%

Source: Maddison Project Database (MPD) 2020 with authors calculations.

and eventually creates a frenzy, capital investment slows as the capital stock deployed in the earlier era continues to provide service and generate income. In the current period, capital deepening has failed, thus far, to fully capture the recovery experienced in previous deployment periods. The lag in capital deepening is one manifestation of what has been labeled "secular stagnation" (Summers 2014).

Table 2.4 shows the well-known productivity slowdown across the table's bottom row. The robust 2.6 percent productivity growth in the Third Industrial Revolution deployment slowed to 2.0 percent per year in the installation period in the Fourth Industrial Revolution. In the current period, productivity growth has slowed even further to an annual rate of 0.9 percent. Again, another sign of failure of the deployment period to launch.

For the United States, Romer showed per capita GDP growth rates increasing steadily over five subperiods between 1800 and 1978 (see Table 2.5). The subperiods approximately coincide with periods of industrial revolution.

Table 2.3 Capital deepening by industrial revolution

	Capital Deepening Capital–Labor Ratios (Thousands of 2012 Dollars per Worker) And Growth Rates							
Industrial Revolution	3rd Era Age of Oil, Automobiles, and Mass Production 1945–1974			4th Era Age of Information and Telecommunications 1971–2010			4th Era Age of Information and Telecommunications 2010–2019	
	Deployment Period			Installation Period			Deployment Period	
	1943	1959	1974	1971	1987	2007	2010	2019
Capital–Labor Ratio	141.0	197.5	261.1	273.1	308.0	414.9	424.2	474.1
Annual Growth Rate	—	—	2.0%	—	—	1.2%	—	1.2%

Source: U.S. Bureau of Economic Analysis. Fixed Assets Accounts Table. Table 1.1 Current-cost net stock of fixed assets and consumer durable goods, row 1, U.S. Bureau of Labor Statistics, All Employees: Total Nonfarm Payrolls, Thousands of Persons, Annual, Seasonally Adjusted and Producer Price Index by Commodity: All Commodities.

Table 2.4 *Labor productivity growth by industrial revolution*

	Labor Productivity Nonfarm Sector Output Per Hour (Base Year 2009 = 100)							
Industrial Revolution	3rd Era Age of Oil, Automobiles, and Mass Production 1945–1974			4th Era Age of Information and Telecommunications 1971–2010			4th Era Age of Information and Telecommunications 2010–2019	
	Deployment Period			Installation Period			Deployment Period	
	1947	1959	1974	1971	1987	2007	2010	2019
Index	23.5	32..6	47.4	45.2	58.6	91.6	99.2	107.9
Annual Growth Rate	—	—	2.6%	—	—	2.0%	—	0.9%

Source: U.S. Bureau of Labor Statistics, Nonfarm Labor Productivity, Major Sector Productivity and Costs, Index, 2009 Base Year = 100.

Capital Investment and the Age of Capital

The surges and plunges of innovation, productivity, and economic growth has capital deepening at its heart. The long-lived nature of capital and capital's technology embodiment, together, suggest change occurs over the long term. With data limited to the most recent hundred years, Figure 2.3 shows the pace of growth in U.S. private nonresidential net investment, including both tangible and intangible capital, over the period 1925 to the present. Aligned with the Third and Fourth Industrial Revolutions, the Great Depression of the 1930s and the 2008–2009 Great Recession and financial crisis are clearly reflected as slowdowns in investment growth. The expansion period of 1943–1974, as shown in Table 2.3, is also apparent, as is the slower growth in the early 21st century.

Figure 2.4 shows nonfarm business sector labor productivity growth over the 1947–2019 period. The well-known productivity growth strength is apparent in the 1947–1970 period, delivering the fruits of the third industrial era. An extended period of weak growth follows as the existing third industrial era capital stock matured and the fourth era was in its early stages. The growth burst in the 1990s accompanied the frenzy

Table 2.5 U.S. per capita GDP growth rates with intervals and growth rates as presented by Romer

Industrial Revolution	Romer's U.S. Per Capita GDP Growth Rates			
	Installation Period		Deployment Period	
	Years	Per Capita GDP Growth	Years	Per Capita GDP Growth
1st	1800–1840	0.58%	1840–1880	1.44%
2nd *	1840–1880	1.44%	1880–1920	1.78%
3rd	1920–1960	1.68%	1960–1978	2.47%

Source: Romer (1986, 1009). See Romer's Table 2. Original source data from Maddisson (1979).

* The years defining the Second Industrial Revolution are not fully aligned with Perez (2002).

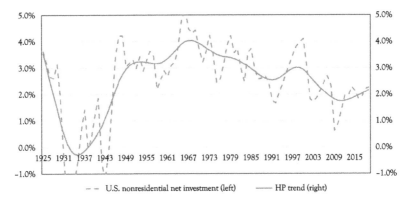

Figure 2.3 U.S. nonresidential investment as a percent of capital stock

Source: U.S. Bureau of Economic Analysis. Fixed Assets Accounts Table. Table 1.1 Current-cost net stock of fixed assets and consumer durable goods, row 4, Table 1.3 Current-cost depreciation of fixed assets and consumer durable goods, row 4, and Table 1.5 Investment in fixed assets and consumer durable goods, row 4.

as the early benefits of the microelectronics era emerged. While the trend has turned positive, in the current period, growth remains weak.

Figure 2.5 shows TFP growth over the 1948–2018 period. Like labor productivity, following an episode of strong growth from 1948 to the early 1970s, growth slowed substantially. The late 1990s growth burst coincided with measurable advances in semiconductor technology and the deployment of restructured computing systems—initially the client–server computing model appeared and soon inexpensive cloud computing

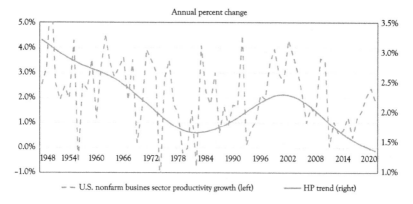

Figure 2.4 U.S. nonfarm business sector productivity growth

Source: U.S. Bureau of Labor Statistics. Major Sector Productivity and Costs, Series Id: PRS85006093, Nonfarm Business Sector, Index, base year = 100, Base Year 2009.

emerged. New software capabilities were also put in place in anticipation of the turn of the century and year 2000. Subsequently, TFP growth has fallen off to record low rates, suggesting full creative destruction has yet to appear (see Hulten 2001).

Fernald writes:

> There was an exceptional IT-induced pace that started after 1995 but that ended around 2004, prior to the Great Recession. The best guess is that we're in a normal/incremental/slow regime now. A back-of-the-envelope projection that assumes productivity growth (net of labor quality growth) will be similar to its 1973–95 pace implies GDP growth of around 1.6 percent. (Fernald 2016, 2)

While two industrial eras do not constitute proof, there are some intriguing dynamics revealed in the limited data set. Many capital assets are long-lived asset with replacement occurring infrequently and with legacy technology and innovation embodied in the capital stock for an extended period. Figure 2.6 shows, as expected, structures have the longest lives while equipment has the shortest, shown in Figure 2.7. Interestingly, however, intellectual property products (IPP)—intangible capital—have lives somewhat longer than equipment.

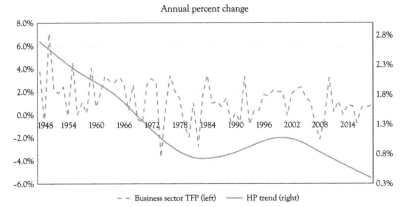

Annual percent change

- - Business sector TFP (left)   —— HP trend (right)

Figure 2.5 U.S. nonfarm total factor productivity growth

Source: John G. Fernald, "A Quarterly, Utilization-Adjusted Series on Total Factor Productivity." FRBSF Working Paper 2012–2019 (updated March 2014). www.johnfernald.net/TFP Produced on March 05, 2020 9:10 AM by John Fernald/Neil Gerstein--fernaldjg@gmail.com (Directory: out\QuarterlyTFP_2020.03.05).Both Figures 2.4 and 2.5 show a transitory productivity revival in the 1995–2004 period. Jorgenson and Stiroh (2000) show that the productivity improvement was a result of improved computing efficiency produced by rapid microprocessor innovation. Computer manufacturers became more efficient at producing units of computing. While the IT-producing sector benefited, IT-users remain in need of additional computing power for advanced AI solutions.

Figure 2.6 also shows that as a result of the dramatic slowing of investment spending growth in the 1930s, the capital stock aged. From an average age of 15.3 years in 1925, the stock grew progressively older to 20.6 years in 1945 and 1946. Clearly, some of the aging could have been a result of neglect while production was focused on the 1941–1945 war effort. However, the average age of the capital stock had already reached 19.5 years in 1940 and 1941 with only one added year of age over the ensuing five years.

Figures 2.6 and 2.7 show, in the 1930–1950 period, the components of the capital stock aged as well. However, in the recent period, equipment and intellectual property products have been renewed with structures and facilities aging substantially. It is the aging capital plant that provided the outdated facilities limiting growth.

As a result of endogenous forces of the Third Industrial Revolution's technologies and postwar demand effects, the aged capital stock of the mid-1940s and the consequent pressure for renewal, contributed to the rapid and aggressive investment of the 1950s to the 1970s. The investment surge ultimately drove the age to a low of 13.8 years in 1986. The

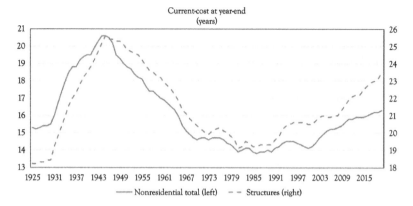

Figure 2.6 *Average age of fixed nonresidential assets—total and structures*

Source: U.S. Bureau of Economic Analysis. Fixed Assets Accounts Table. Table 1.9 Current-cost average age at yearend of fixed assets and consumer durable goods, rows 4, 5, 6, and 7.

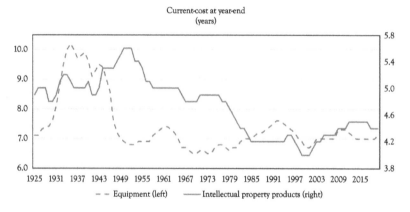

Figure 2.7 *Average age of fixed nonresidential assets—equipment and intellectual property products*

Source: U.S. Bureau of Economic Analysis. Fixed Assets Accounts Table. Table 1.9 Current-cost average age at yearend of fixed assets and consumer durable goods, rows 4, 5, 6, and 7.

subsequent three decades of slower investment spending growth, added three years to the stock's age.

Compared with the prewar capital stock age of 19.5 years in 1940, shown in Figure 2.6, the 16.3-year age in 2020 is largely accounted for by the shift in the composition of capital investment spending, which reflects the increased importance of equipment and IPP in 2020. Figure 2.8 shows the trend in the age of nonresidential net capital investment with the 1940 weights applied. In the absence of the composition shift, the 2020 average capital age would have been 18.9 years, only slightly below its 1940 value. Controlling for the compositional shift, the capital stock in 2020 is about as aged as it was in 1940.

The U.S. capital infrastructure progressed through a 40-year aging process from the late 1960s to late in the first decade of the 21st century. As the period progressed, the overbuilding of the 1960s, during a period of strong demand, put in place a large physical private and public capital stock. As a consequence of the long period of capital deprecation, the stock became increasingly antiqued and less productive.

The technological capability of legacy capital does not respond swiftly to innovation. Rather, because new technology is only effective when new capital is deployed, the prolonged useful life of tangible and intangible capital slows the rate of adjustment. Capital investment is, in part, governed by the long-lived nature of capital. The increasingly rapid capital deepening in the deployment period—most recently 1943 to 1974—sets the stage for a slowdown in capital deepening in the subsequent installation period. As the existing capital depreciates, the previous era's technology matures, and the next generation of technology is birthed, unlocked by endogenous generation of new ideas, innovation, and technology creating increased aggregate demand.

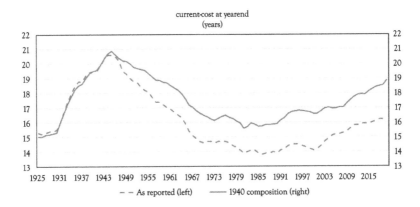

Figure 2.8 Average age of fixed nonresidential assets—as reported and 1940 composition

Source: U.S. Bureau of Economic Analysis. Fixed Assets Accounts Table. Table 1.9 Current-cost average age at yearend of fixed assets and consumer durable goods, rows 4, 5, 6, and 7 with author's calculations.

CHAPTER 3

Four Industrial Revolutions

On January 3, 1842, Charles Dickens and his wife, Catherine, left Liverpool on a 19-day Atlantic crossing to America. After a very cold and stormy winter steamship journey, at the Boston docking, Dickens was just two weeks shy of his 30th birthday. Dickens had already achieved fame and literary success with the 1836 serial publication of *The Pickwick Papers*, the 19th-century version of a 21st-century Internet streaming event. *A Christmas Carol* was soon to be published in 1843.

The six-month American itinerary began with visits to Lowell MA, New York, and Philadelphia, followed by a journey to more than a dozen eastern-American cities, as far south as Richmond, as far west as St. Louis, and as far north as Quebec. Dickens provided a colorful, detailed travel-log of the six months in *American Notes for General Circulation* (Dickens 1842).

A one-day train excursion to Lowell had been prearranged with business leaders of Lowell's factory community. The city of Lowell had been founded a century earlier by Francis Cabot Lowell who sought a blank slate on which to build an entirely new approach to textile manufacturing. Lowell and his business partners had achieved success with the first American integrated textile mill in Waltham, MA. But with the integrated model's success, prices were falling and demand increasing at a faster pace than could be satisfied. Scale was desperately needed. A large undeveloped site was soon discovered at the confluence of the Merrimack and Concord Rivers which was, conveniently, two miles down-river from the 36-foot drop of the Pawtucket Falls.

The geography was perfect for the construction of an elaborate array of canals, which, by the power of gravity, were fed from above the falls and which emptied below the falls. The costless water power, eliminated the dirt and soot of coal power, which had taken on increased importance as an energy source in England. Dickens wrote:

> The very river that moves the machinery in the mills (for they are all worked by water power), seems to acquire a new character from the fresh buildings of bright red brick and painted wood among which it takes its course; and to be as light-headed, thoughtless, and brisk a young river, in its murmurings and tumblings, as one would desire to see. (Dicken 1842, Chapter 4)

With the construction of the canal network, massive financial capital was raised. Investors were intrigued with the entirely new manufacturing approach. The construction of a widespread complex of textile manufacturing facilities soon appeared, all while the technology of textile manufacturing, itself, was rapidly advancing.

While Dickens was clearly impressed by the young city's "quaintness and oddity of character," the massive manufacturing facilities, and the leading-edge technology, he was much more impressed with the novel use of human resources—"the mill girls."

Dickens was very much aware of the hard work endured by the young women. With 12-hour days and 6-day weeks, the work was not easy. However, the mills provided, according to Dickens, a clean, comfortable environment with "much fresh air," "conveniences for washing," and windows with green plants to reduce the sun's warming, greenhouse effect. Dickens described the young women as well-dressed, carrying themselves with pride and self-respect.

The living arrangements were also of interest to Dickens. The women lived in boarding houses provided by the business leaders. Dickens described the living arrangement and security as if a nineteenth century #me-too movement already protected the young women from threat and assault. Health care was provided in a novel arrangement with a hospital located some distance from the mills and boarding houses.

However, what was perhaps most intriguing to Dickens was the artistic and literary life of women factory workers. Dickens wrote:

> I am now going to state three facts, which will startle a large class of readers on this [British] side of the Atlantic, very much. Firstly, there is a joint-stock piano in a great many of the boarding-houses. Secondly, nearly all these young ladies subscribe to circulating libraries. Thirdly, they have got up among themselves a periodical called *The Lowell Offering*, "A repository of original articles, written exclusively by females actively employed in the mills,"—which is duly printed, published, and sold; and whereof I brought away from Lowell four hundred good solid pages, which I have read from beginning to end. (Dickens 1842, Chapter 4)

After that thorough, careful reading, Dickens concluded: "putting entirely out of sight the fact of the articles having been written by these girls after the arduous labours of the day, that it will compare advantageously with a great many English Annuals" (Dickens 1842, Chapter 4).

The story of Dickens' journey to America and his one-day visit to Lowell highlights several important elements that have had enduring importance across each industrial revolution. The advances in technology and massive tangible capital investment requirements are apparent in the Lowell story and each industrial revolution. The story also highlights the role of falling prices, the appearance of rapidly increasing demand, the need for scale, the benefit of business model innovation, and the opportunity for new energy sources. However, Dickens's writing also points to the critical role of human resources. The innovative notion of attracting bright, intelligent, young women to work in textile manufacturing, for a time at least, helped to meet the demand for labor. The truly creative aspect of the arrangement was to offer an arrangement that deeply engaged the women in their work, secured their living arrangement, and promoted their leisure. Worker engagement, good or bad, is an important element of each industrial revolution.

However, what a one-day visit misses is the dynamics of change as the technology matures, capital investment accumulates, and demand is satisfied. The story of industrial revolution is ultimately about the pressures

Table 3.1 Industrial revolutions eras

Four Industrial Revolutions						
		Installation		Global financial markets crisis	Deployment	
		Eruption	Frenzy		Synergy	Maturity
1	Age of steam and railways	1829	Panic 1847		• Standards on gauge, time • Catalog sales companies 1873 • Economies of scale	
2	Age of steel, electricity, and heavy engineering	1875	Depression 1893		• Urban development • Support for interventionism 1920	
3	Age of oil, automobiles, and mass production	1908	Crash 1929		• Build-out of interstate highways 1974 • IMF, World Bank, BIS	
4	Age of information and telecommunications	1971	2008–2009 Great recession		• Potential deployment period ahead	

Source: Perez (2002), 78.

and dislocation necessary to force migration from one era to another (see Table 3.1).

This chapter provides an overview of each industrial revolution from an economist's perspective. Notwithstanding long-standing debates among economic historians about the nature of industrial revolutions, the aim here is to provide an economists' view on what has been largely an economic historians' discussion on whether these are "revolutions" or "evolutions" and what the necessary preconditions are.

The First Industrial Revolution: Creating the Factory System

As the First Industrial Revolution began, a series of inventions resulted in the appearance of the British factory system (Landes 1969). After a string of innovations, the factory system fundamentally altered business and work. Machines were substituted for human skill and effort. A new, more efficient energy source—steam—were created. And, new and abundant raw materials—wool, cotton, and iron ore—appeared. By the early 19th century, the installation period of the First Industrial Revolution had taken hold. Economic activity and knowledge were growing fast enough to create and support the needed capital investment and technological innovation.

While the first revolution began in England, it soon spread to Scotland, Wales, and Ireland, as well as North America, most notably New England.

Per capita incomes were rising and the technology provided a means to substantially lower prices of goods for which there was elastic demand. As new technology and innovative business processes resulted in lower prices, the number of units sold grew more than proportionately. Revenue grew rapidly. Massive capital investments materialized in both Britain and New England. Light woolen and cotton textiles were provided to meet, first, domestic demand and soon global demand. The notion of workers and families having access to an expanding wardrobe, beyond everyday work clothes, was at the leading edge of technological change.

While water power was sufficient for early textile manufacturing, a more powerful and efficient source was required for the development of a productive iron industry, producing at scale. With abundant coal deposits in both England and North America, coal became the preferred energy source. After 20 years of development, from 1830 to 1850, the steam engine with coal as the energy source, provided sufficient power for a highly efficient iron industry. The coal–steam combination permitted, but did not cause, the development and diffusion of the First Industrial Revolution.

Like success of the coal–steam combination, the advent of the rail network in England and across Europe and North America further aided the development and diffusion of the first revolution. With prices of goods falling and access to larger rail-provided markets, economies of scale in production improved the economics of production for a much broader array of businesses, employing a much larger labor force. The rail network also altered the competitive landscape as entrepreneurs had a wider choice of locations from which to operate and sell product.

However, as the installation period of the First Industrial Revolution progressed, business leaders and workers resisted. Despite the benefits of the new technology and the growth in demand for their products, resistance was strong. As Landes writes, "only the strongest incentives could have persuaded entrepreneurs to undertake and accept these changes; and only major advantages could have overcome the dogged resistance of labor to the very principle of mechanization" (Landes 1969, 43). However, entrepreneurs soon discovered that with rising demand, marginal costs were rising as well. The inadequacy of the legacy technology created pressure for improvement. It didn't take long for entrepreneurs to learn that the reduction in cost resulting from the new system would sufficiently cover the expense of the needed investment in the new capital and technology. Despite the powerful business case of growth and expansion, entrepreneurs now faced a new risk environment. Where previously, manufacturing costs consisted primarily of labor and materials, financed from current period cash flow, now fixed costs in the form of capital investment appeared. Fixed costs were a new source of entrepreneurial risk. With new long-term debt necessary, judgments were required about business profitability years in advance.

For workers, the new business model—the factory system—meant a separation of work from the means of production. The worker no longer had to be both entrepreneur and worker. The small, artisanal enterprise could be replaced, should the worker choose, with a week's work with defined hours, pay, and responsibilities. The worker could leave the pressures of building and managing a business to someone else. The trade-off was that the factory system imposed a new form of discipline under the watchful eye of the factory overseer (See Crafts and Mills 2002a and 2002b).

While data are limited, Landes estimates that by 1830 there were "hundreds of thousands of men, women, and children employed" in the British factory system (Landes 1969, 114). Importantly, factory production created new tasks and new opportunities for workers and businesses that had not previously existed. Machine building and maintenance were newly and frequently subcontracted to those with specialized skills. Completely new occupations were created. Increased capital investment, employment growth, and the appearance of new tasks and new businesses, all contributed to substantial macroeconomic benefits as income and wealth grew rapidly.

As we saw in the previous chapter, the need for massive capital investment for both the factory system and the railroads not only led to the attraction of massive financial capital but soon to a frenzy in the financial markets. The prospects of future profits became, for the first time, an opportunity for third-party investors who hoped for substantial capital gains and income growth.[1] Not surprisingly, enterprise values became

---

[1] Landes describes the widening available of bank credit and services as well as the rise of joint-stock commercial banks. See Landes (1969), pp. 206–210.

disconnected from reality. However, after the 1857 London financial markets correction, battered investors were more informed and better prepared to fund activities by entrepreneurs with a shared view of future opportunities. With financial capital available and resistance to change and transformation overcome, the now GPT was available to support creative destruction in the decades ahead.

Thus, the deployment period of the First Industrial Revolution, from 1850 to 1873, was a period of unprecedented growth with incomes across the United Kingdom, United States, and Europe rising rapidly. As would be expected in a deployment period, these were also years of technological maturity. The technologies first developed in Britain, and later in the United States, spread across Europe and North America. The third quarter of the 19th century was a period of sustained creativity and important innovation.

Institutional change was especially important. With knowledge diffusion and the absorptive capacity of those receiving the newly emerging technological expertise increasingly important, easier conditions for company formation was a critical change in the rules of business governance and management. Britain was the first nation to permit the right to limited liability formation by simple registration (Landes 1969, 198). Despite an initial fear of unlimited speculation, concerns were soon overcome and the true limited liability partnership become available across much of Europe. Other changes such as the end of the prohibition of usury, the creation of transactions executed by bank check, the easing of penalties for debt and bankruptcy, and the amendment of patent laws to allow for trademarks and other intangible forms for business property, all eased the adoption of the new technology and new business models. As is characteristic of deployment periods, not only did the mature technology spread widely and tangible and intangible capital investment accelerate but also the rules of the game changed among businesses, governments, and families.

Importantly, the first revolution's deployment period brought improvements in transportation, increased availability of new energy sources and raw materials, and increased access to financial capital. The deployment period also brought a creative entrepreneurial response to the long-run opportunity and to the short-run improved facilitation of business creation, knowledge diffusion, and tangible and intangible capital investment.

Unlike the installation period when British firms dominated markets and technology, in the deployment period, a much broader set of competitors emerged—both across Europe and the United States. Not surprisingly, across Europe, barriers to international trade fell with riverway levies lower, exchange rates simplified, and a series of treaties between nations signed. The United States was endowed with abundant land and natural resources, which caused labor scarcity but resulted in capital complementary (see Habakkuk 1962 and Broadberry 1997). By the 1870s, all nations saw their exports grow. With the added competition, home industries did not collapse but grew stronger as marginally inefficient firms disappeared with business reallocated to more efficient firms.

By 1870, Landes observes, "British industry had exhausted the gains implicit in the original cluster of innovations that had constituted the Industrial Revolution ... Not until a series of major advances opened new areas of investment around the turn of the [twentieth] century was this deceleration reversed" (Landes 1969, 234–235). Importantly, demand failed to keep up with very rapidly growing industry capacity. Excess capacity substantially reduced the need for further capital investment. With a growing array of suppliers, demand was easily met. New customers with unmet needs were much harder to find. Landes writes:

> There were customers for those who knew how to find them; but one had to look for them in new places and woo them in new ways. And the task was not so easy as it had been for the pioneer industrialists of the first half of the century. (Landes 1969, p. 237)

The First Industrial Revolution had exhausted its opportunity and its deployment period was coming to an end.

The Second Industrial Revolution: Electric Power Creates Expansion

As the Second Industrial Revolution began, the legacy of the First Industrial Revolution hung over it. The success of the preceding period had put in place what was, by the last quarter of the 19th century, an aging technology embedded in an aging and excessive capital stock governed by business rules and practices from the earlier era. However, the deployment period of the previous era had also created great wealth. The resulting golden age has been called *La Belle Époque* when Europe achieved its greatest power in global politics, and exerted its maximum global influence.[2] The epic coincided with the installation period of the Second Industrial Revolution. Not surprisingly, income and wealth protection became important motivators in resisting change.

Slower growth in capital investment along with continued income growth and wealth accumulation is characteristic of the installation period. The stock of capital put in place in the prior era is sufficiently large that it continues to generate income and wealth even as growth is slowing. Despite the capital investment slowdown, as the name implies, the installation period is one in which new technology is installed, initially on an experimental basis with immature applications. The development of the new technology is setting the stage for the possibility of growth in a future period.

Advances realized in the early adoption of electricity were at the heart of the installation period of the Second Industrial Revolution. The advent of electric power permitted the birth of electric motors, organic chemistry and synthetics, the internal-combustion engine, automotive equipment, precision manufacturing, and assembly (Landes 1969, 235). These advances made possible an entirely new set of consumer goods—the sewing machine, inexpensive clocks, the bicycle, electric lighting, and electric appliances. Robert Gordon describes, at length, the impact that these innovations had on consumers and families. Gordon explores the increase in living standards and welfare as a result of water and sewer service, indoor bathrooms, central heating, lighting, and early appliances (Gordon 2016, Chapter 4).

The new technology, and the products it spawned, altered the demand for capital investment significantly. Where the First Industrial Revolution was one in which investment surged primarily for capital goods, most

---

[2] (See Wikipedia: *Belle Époque* https://en.wikipedia.org/wiki/Belle_%C3%89 poque).

notably for textile equipment, metals production, and railways, the Second Industrial Revolution created demand for capital investment for consumer goods. The demand shift and the new technology suggests that as the installation period of the Second Industrial Revolution progressed, and consumer goods production at scale was possible, the existing capital infrastructure was antiquated and poorly suited for the decades ahead. Entering the installation period of the Second Industrial Revolution, capital infrastructure would have to be renewed to meet the needs of the new consumer.

The technological innovation of the Second Industrial Revolution has been well documented by Paul David, including the "war of the currents" between Thomas Edison and George Westinghouse in establishing alternating current as the industry standard, building the electrical power network, and setting global standards (see David 1990 and 1998). In addition, Nordhaus (1997) details, in a well-known paper, lighting innovations over millennia. Among the many innovations that have reduced the price of lighting by many orders of magnitude, the development of electric power and the carbon-filament lamp were among the most important.

By the third quarter of the 19th century, the new technologies were beginning to have a broader social, as well as economic, impact. While it was very beneficial to workers and families to have the access to an expanded and affordable wardrobe that inexpensive textiles provided in the First Industrial Revolution, electric power technology had a much broader and more consequential impact.

The broad social and economic benefits that the advent of electric power brought can be seen in the Swiss experience. In recent work, Brey (2021) has provided new insight at the outset of the installation period of the Second Industrial Revolution.[3]

Switzerland was early to adopt electric power in the late 19th century. Because the generation of electric power relied exclusively on locally

---

[3] Brey finds persistent differences across the Swiss regions with early access to electric power, not because of the manner in which electricity is used but as a result of increased human capital accumulation and innovation. Brey had access to Swiss data covering the period from 1860 to 2011, so is able to consider both the installation of the technology in the late 1800s and the long-run consequences. Importantly, the installation of electric power generation was unique in Switzerland and had the effect of creating a random control experiment from which Brey can draw conclusions about causality.

available waterpower, the initial ability to adopt electricity depended on unique geographic features, randomly distributed across the nation. In addition, waterpower was unexploitable with earlier power technologies. In effect, waterpower suddenly appeared and was spread randomly across Swiss regions for a 20-year period. Thus, a natural experiment was created.

Brey finds that industries associated with the provision of electricity provided a meaningful boost to industrialization in the 1860–1880 period, as well as a positive effect on economic development over the long run. The reason for stronger economic performance, Brey finds, is that the early electric power exposure triggered the accumulation of human capital and further innovation, leading to persistent divergence in economic development. Local schoolchildren immediately experienced an improvement in educational outcomes with (1) the student population expanding more rapidly in areas adopting electricity earlier, (2) employers and local governments providing apprenticeships and technical schools, and (3) increased support in national referendums for education investment. Those early adopting areas today remain innovative with a higher patenting rate.

As the Swiss deployment of electric power suggests, deep business and social innovation followed the Second Industrial Revolution's technological innovation. One important innovation, as documented by Alfred Chandler is the creation of the modern industrial enterprise in the deployment period of the Second Industrial Revolution. As expected, the 1893–1920 deployment period is a time in which the power of creative destruction fundamentally altered the organization of business and work. Chandler finds that those business leaders who were able to fully exploit the potential of the then-new electric power technology made investments large enough to develop "competitive capabilities that permitted their enterprises and their nations' industries to dominate markets abroad as well as at home" (Chandler 1998, 432).[4] Chandler argues that exploitation of the new technology resulted in the creation of the modern

---

[4] Harberger (1998) developed the notion of "yeasty" growth during the same period Chandler (1998) was documenting the "modern industrial enterprise." Both captured the essence of the deployment period. Chandler provided an empirical view of an important new turn-of-the-century business model, while Harberger articulated a theoretical notion of more rapid deployment period growth following innovation and transformation.

industrial enterprise, citing investment in (1) production large enough to generate economies of scale and scope that the new technology had potential to deliver, (2) marketing and distribution capabilities large enough to sell products in the volume produced, and (3) managerial skill and structure to manage, coordinate, and allocate resources for future production and distribution.

Not only did such enterprises appear suddenly in the last quarter of the 19th century, Chandler writes, but they also clustered in industries with common characteristics. These industry-leading enterprises were found in food, chemicals, oil, primary metals, electrical machinery, and transportation equipment. They were produced in volume and in a capital-intensive environment. And, they were located principally in Britain, Germany, and the United States. Notable clusters appeared in cigarettes, tires, newsprint, plate and flat glass, razor blades, and mass-produced cameras. In today's lexicon, such enterprises are called "superstar firms" (see Autor et al. 2020). Chandler observes that high-volume electric power generation in the 1880s resulted in massive capital investment and created needs and opportunities for technological and organization innovation across many industries.

Beyond the "superstar firms," described by Chandler, the very slowly changing behavior of the nonsuperstar firms—those with lagging innovation, diminished competitiveness, and lack of technological intensity—arose from deeply rooted cultural barriers. Lazonick (1998) argues that after the deployment of the electric power network, some British industrialists were challenged to develop the organizational capabilities that Chandler had observed elsewhere. These British business leaders, like craft workers, jealously guarded the status quo.

In addition to the absence of adaptive British leadership skills, Lazonick highlights barriers that proved difficult to overcome—the durability of then-existing plant and equipment, the immobility of workers, a lack of understanding of the new science and technology, the embedded class structure making it difficult for senior leaders to gain commitment and coordination of technical specialists, and the failure to restructure the education system to marry science and technology.

For previously successful business leaders of the earlier period, Lazonick asserts, "the strategy of living off his industrial capital was rational." The required dramatic transformation of the social determinants

of technological progress was beyond the lived experience. As the Second
Industrial Revolution began, fixed costs—and thus risk—were limited,
inputs were readily available, outputs were sold in a known marketplace,
and competition was nearby and well understood.

With success as an individual business, not as a "modern industrial
corporation" with the beginnings of global reach, Lazonick (1998) and
Landes (1969) point to a changed strategic and operating model. Lazonick
writes the British business leaders' "estimates of returns were conservative
because [their] organized competitors had the power to shape their economic environment in ways that [the British leader], as an individual
proprietor, could not."

In contrast to the British experience, as the Second Industrial Revolution began, Germany was well positioned to prosper. During the first
three-quarters of the 19th century, Germany addressed transportation,
communication, and political barriers across a collection of independent
and sovereign territories, allowing for commercial and financial success
and a strengthening of institutional rules and practices. In addition,
Tilly and Kopsidis find that increased literacy, school enrollment, and
patent activity contributed to Germany's "take-off." In addition, they
observe that the high literacy rates also contributed to the spread of new
technical knowledge and high numbers of skilled craftsmen (Tilly and
Kopsidis, 2020, 142–143).[5] By the last quarter of the 19th century, Germany emerged as an industrial power (Tilly and Kopsidis, 2020, 165).
The railway boom created important points of linkage between heavy
industry and mechanical engineering allowing for information exchange
and knowledge spillover as the new technology was adopted. Aided by
the abundant supply of literate and skilled workers, the close relationship
between science and industry resulted in substantial research and development activity in pigments and dyestuff, forming an important link in the
chain of chemical processes for textiles, leather, plastic, paper, packaging,

---

[5] Similarly, Gordon finds that by the last quarter of the 19th century education
practices in the United States were comparable to those of the "major relatively
rich European nations." Gordon writes: "Native-born Americans were largely
literate by 1870, and the remaining cases of illiteracy involved immigrants to the
northern states or former black slaves in the south" (Gordon 2016, p. 58).

printing inks, paints and polymers, and so on. As a result, over the Second Industrial Revolution's deployment period, production of pharmaceuticals, synthetic fertilizers, and other heavy chemical products expanded rapidly. In addition, building on the newly available electric power technology, industry giants such as Siemens and AEG emerged in the nascent electrical engineering industry (Tilly and Kopsidis, 2020, 175).

Consequently, a regime shift occurred with American, Swiss, and German businesses taking the lead. Landes asserts that "the rapid industrial expansion of a unified Germany was the most important development of the half century that preceded the First World War" (Landes 1969, 326). The new innovative and competitive landscape included global competition, the power of corporate enterprises, research and development of new productive resources, the interaction of organization and technology, the required human resources, and the commitment of financial resources. British business leaders were challenged to adapt. As industrial leadership passed from Britain to Germany in the closing decades of the 19th century, Germany's gains, according to Landes, were social and institutional. Britain, Landes writes, "basked complacently in the sunset of economic hegemony." Family firm ownership was passed down to generations with less skill, knowledge, and interest. Reflecting amateurism and complacency, corporate enterprises recruited inexperienced leaders and promoted leaders out of production roles ill prepared for larger challenges. German entrepreneurs, by contrast, were trained in science and the new technology, worked hard, and were astute financial managers. While older British enterprises were complacent, younger firms failed to appear in larger enough numbers in the new industries of electrical engineering and organic chemistry (Landes 1969, 336–338).

The early decades of the 20th century, as expected in the deployment phase, brought broad advances that indicated approaching maturity. Basic innovations spread from small groups of "superstar firms" to the balance of the business sector with electric power used widely. While new uses and less expensive power promoted capital formation, the importance of intangible capital cannot be overemphasized. Scientific knowledge, technical skill, and high standards of performance weighted heavily. Nonetheless, aggressive capital investment in both Britain and Germany eventually resulted in capacity outstripping demand. With the technology maturing, capacity in surplus, and the world at war, the Second Industrial Revolution came to an end.

The Third Industrial Revolution: War and Depression Ignites Growth

As the Third Industrial Revolution began, the global economy faced unprecedented problems and challenges. The 20th century had already brought a world war and a simultaneous global pandemic, both resulting in extraordinary death and destruction. The installation period of the Third Industrial Revolution has become more commonly known as the interwar years, as it was bookended by a world war and a pandemic juxtaposed to a second world war and a global depression. As the era began, early in the 20th century, the United States was assuming global economic leadership after a period of strong growth and success in the Second Industrial Revolution.

The First World War hastened the dissolution of the international economic order of the prior revolutionary period. Britain ended free and open trade with the institution of a 33⅓ percent tariff on trading partners, except those in the empire; the monetary stability of the prior century disappeared; and global inflation resulted from emergency conditions, market quotas, and rationing. After the war, German inflation was especially severe with the Allied nations imposing burdens of reconstruction that were extracted a very high price (Landes 1969, 357–364).

With the hangover from the preceding deployment era and consequences of the global financial impact of the war's conclusion, the Third Industrial Revolution's installation period not only suffered from global inflation but also weak employment growth. In today's language, it was a period of stagflation. Despite constraints imposed on European nations with the liquidation of financial assets held abroad to pay for the war, opportunities in the energy and automotive industries began to appear with mass production emerging as an entirely new production model. German and U.S. capital investment was growing rapidly.

By the early 20th century, as series of automotive design and mechanical improvements created a more useful and usable vehicle, opening the possibility of mass production. Steering improved; engines were larger;

and spark plugs, carburetors, transmissions, and starters all made automobiles more reliable and convenient. These innovations expanded the market with greater consumer interest in an easier-to-use vehicle. Consequently, production at scale became an important opportunity. Henry Ford and others soon began the development of the internal-combustion engine and the mass production of automobiles. Other industries also adopted the same assembly and production model (Gordon 2016, 150). As a means of travel, auto travel began to replace walking, mass transit, and horse-drawn wagons. Aircraft manufacturing and airplane travel also gained traction as the installment period progressed. While remaining very immature, initial attempts were made to make air travel economic.

Not only did transportation begin to improve but communications became more widely available. By 1919, rotary dial telephones and automatic switches were introduced into service (Gordon 2016, 183). Radio technology also gained, in part as a result of the war and in part as a result of the invention of the vacuum tube. The tube's innovation made possible not only the radio but also radar, recording devices, the computer, automated control systems, and television (Landes 1969, 425).

Consumers also benefited as families were no longer limited to purchasing from small local stores. The A&P grocery chain began its period of most rapid expansion in 1912. The Kroger and Grand Union chains soon followed. Volume purchases by the chains allowed them to pass on lower prices to consumers, creating a meaningful threat to small independent merchants. Urban, general merchandise department stores soon followed (Gordon 2016, 78–90).

In the Third Industrial Revolution's installation period, as expected, new technology—internal-combustion engine, telephone systems, vacuum tubes—appeared but with slow adoption, outdated business models, and technologically lagging enterprises. Landes summarizes the pressures to transform as the installment period progressed:

> It was the more progressive, more innovative branches that grew fastest and drew redundant labour from lagging sectors. For another, this movement of workers conduced to higher wages for those who remained, so that it paid to substitute capital for labor. The result was a stimulus to technological improvement in these

lagging sectors, which in turn hastened the purge of inefficient enterprises and the process of reallocation. Prosperity may be the best friend of progress, only because new investment usually entails new and better ways of doing things. (Landes 1969, 420–421)

The coming of the new technology spawned rapid investment in UK, Germany, and U.S. tangible and intangible capital. Along with a massive flow of funds into the equity shares, frantic speculation on share exchanges was the eventual result. By late 1928 and early 1929, American banks began calling their European loans. When the net export of capital plunged, European banks came under great pressure. A rapid fall in the price of industrial equity shares, quickly set off market reaction with equity values crashing. In the scramble for cash, loans and debts were recalled. The lack of capital quickly resulted in a business collapse and rising unemployment. The Great Recession had begun and the installation period of the Third Industrial Revolution came to an end.

The Great Depression, as is well known, was a global event. However, Germany was affected as much or more than any national economy. With high inflation and onerous war retribution payments extracted by the allied nations, depressed business conditions, and massive unemployment created polarization between an extreme left and an extreme right. With the coming of the National Socialist party, irrational beliefs and rise of Hitler's government, by 1939–1940, preparation for war was complete.

The death and destruction resulting from the second world war created an enormous hole in Europe's private and public physical capital infrastructure. In the United States, the impact of the war was very different. No measurable military action occurred on the U.S. mainland and no capital was destroyed. Instead, the U.S. economy was converted to a war-time footing and economic activity and business processes were widely employed to produce military output. As a result, when the war concluded, U.S. and European businesses were left with a decision to return to the prewar technology and business processes or to replace their military production with the then more modern, current technology. Similarly, the workforce was fundamentally transformed as well. Those serving in the military learned new skills and a new way of life while those not joining military service—most often women—joined the workforce for the first time and also gained new skills and experience.

The shock of the Great Depression cleansed nonperforming assets—both equity and debt—from investor's balance sheets and freed capital for more productive use. The reallocation of labor and capital from inefficient and lagging firms, the business sector dislocation created by the Second World War, and the transformation of the workforce as a result of military and wartime activity, all combined to set the stage for very strong economic growth and more equally distributed incomes in the period immediately ahead. A very painful 15 years, experienced worldwide, was about to pay-off with 30 years of prosperity.

In understanding the means by which the benefits of the deployment period of the Third Industrial Revolution appeared, Landes cites four "prime moves" and enduring factors: an increase in technical and scientific knowledge, a new spirit of international cooperation, an increase in economic knowledge (by which he seems to mean improved business leadership and more skilled public policy making), and a postwar commitment to change and growth (Landes 1969, 536).

Growing out of innovation of the technology initially employed in radio, television, and radar devices, computing machines became a reality. Despite their initially primitive nature and lack of electronic componentry, basic business functions were eventually performed at scale by early computers. In the later portion of the deployment period electronic components became a reality, setting the stage for the GPT of the Fourth Industrial Revolution.

Similarly, the chemical industry built on its advances of the installation period created artificial fibers, leather substitutes, plastics, protective coatings, new drugs, and nylon, the first all-synthetic fiber. Other industries brought products to market such as in optics, photography, xerography, light metals, and nuclear power (Landes 1969, 514–517).

Consequently, a question subject to debate for many years surrounds the possible link between the cognitive acceleration in the Third Industrial Revolution's installation period and economic growth experienced in the deployment period. While Landes's work occurred too early in the era to expect an answer, with the benefit of 50 additional years of data, Gordon follows Landes in exploring the same question. In Gordon's view, there are several elements that explain the strong growth in the 1950s and 1960s:

- The Second World War created an "economic rescue" along every conceivable dimension from education and the GI Bill to the deficit-financed mountain of household saving that gave a new middle class the ability to purchase the consumer durables that had been unavailable during the war.
- On the supply side, the U.S. government paid for vast expansion of the capital stock for new factories and equipment that were then operated by private firms to create aircraft, ships, and weapons.
- The surge in infrastructure investment in the 1930s and 1940s, related to depression recovery programs and the Second World War, provided for more efficient movement of people, goods, and power. These projects included, for example, building the nation's highway system, the Golden Gate Bridge, the Bay Bridge, the Tennessee Valley Authority, and the Hoover Dam.
- Finally, another supply channel Gordon cites is "learning by doing." As a result of supply constraints imposed by the war effort in 1942 to 1945, each firm found it necessary to devise new techniques to boost output while constrained by limited capital and labor resources (Gordon 2016, 535–565).

Landes writes that the greatest change of all was a "revolution in expectations and values." The revolution created a return to "the high hopes of the dawn of industrialization, to the buoyant optimism of those first generations of English innovators" (Landes 1969, 536).

The strong growth of the 1950s and 1960s eventually gave way to the 1970s slower growth, bringing the Third Industrial Revolution to an end. By the late 1960s, demand exceeded available capacity with U.S. imports growing rapidly, demand that domestic producers were unable to address. When combined with a series of policy errors by the

Nixon Administration and the Federal Reserve, historically high inflation resulted with slower growth following.

Perhaps the best illustration of the early 1970s inflection point is the 1971 pressure on the Nixon Administration to the address of the value of the dollar, exchange rates, and the gold standard. After the protectionism of the 1930s, the world's finance leaders agreed at the 1944 Bretton Woods conference to fix the value of one ounce of gold at $35. Other currencies were fixed to the dollar within a trading band. Any government or central bank could redeem their dollars by going to the gold window at the U.S. Treasury. For 25 years, the dollar stood at the center of an institutional arrangement that was an important contributor to robust U.S. economic growth and the astounding recovery in Europe and Japan. However, the arrangement was under severe pressure as the Third Industrial Revolution was about to come to an end. Indeed, by 1971 the U.S. Treasury was short of gold, putting at risk the role of the dollar.[6] With the dollar, as the world's global currency and the need for much of the world to hold dollars, the United States benefited with lower interest rates and ready access to capital for financing government spending. Jeffery Garten tells the story of this policy inflection point in some detail (Garten 2021).

While most crises seem to appear out of nowhere, rapidly rising inflation and a growing trade deficit—both at least partially linked to the overexpansion of capital investment—had created a series of currency crises leading up to 1971. A stable dollar was at risk. Despite a series of global finance leader summits convened to save the post-World War II currency arrangement, by mid-1972, floating exchange rates had become the norm. Each industrial revolution gets to define its own set of rules, practices, and arrangements. The next and Fourth Industrial Revolution was about to get its chance.

---

[6] By 1971, gold had been draining from the U.S. Treasury for many years. In 1955, the United States had $2.7 billion of gold at $35 per ounce to cover the $13.5 billion of liabilities to other governments and central banks, 60 percent more than required. By mid-1971, the U.S. stock of gold had increased to $10.2 billion with official dollar holdings by foreign governments exploding to $40 billion. To make good on its commitment to exchange gold for dollars, the United States had only 25 percent of what would be needed (Garten 2021, p. 9–10).

Beyond the high and rising inflation, capacity limitations, and the crumpling institutional arrangements, the era's technology developed in the 1920s and 1930s reached maturity, having been fully exploited for nearly five decades. The result was a need to turn the page. Like earlier revolutionary periods, the move to a new era, initially, had to come to grips with the legacy of the concluding era and, at the same time, find new technologies to support future growth.

The Fourth Industrial Revolution: Resistance and Computing

The beginning of the Fourth Industrial Revolution coincided with the invention of the microprocessor. In 1974, Intel introduced the 8080, called a "computer on a chip." However, it was more than 20 years before Intel and others achieved sufficient scale for the microprocessor to have a measurable impact on growth.

The legacy of the Third Industrial Revolution's deployment period hung over the installation period of the Fourth Industrial Revolution for a considerable period. The inflation of the late 1960s and early 1970s continued and worsened throughout the entire decade of the 1970s. As is well known, it was not until Paul Volcker was appointed as Chair of the Federal Reserve Board in 1979, that monetary policy succeeded in addressing the worsening inflation problem. Under Volcker's leadership, the Fed fundamentally transformed the execution of monetary policy, and imposed extremely tight financial conditions on global financial markets that inflation began to lessen. Nearly six years was required to achieve the Fed's inflation goals. Ironically, in creating the new monetary policy arrangement, it was also Paul Volcker who, a decade earlier, had played a critical analytical and support role as the Nixon Administration came to grips with the collapsing global institutional currency arrangement.

The increased use of fossil fuels, and oil in particular, was also a legacy of the Third Industrial Revolution. Consequently, the installation period of the Fourth Industrial Revolution was a period of extreme oil price volatility as demand surged and energy investment responded to changing price signals. The West Texas Intermediate (WTI) oil price rose from $22.39 in June 1973 to $134.22 in May 1980, a more than six-time increase in just nine months, before wiping out the enter gain, falling back over

18 years to $20.44 in December 1998. The WTI price rose again, over 20 years, to $177.80 in June 2008 but fell to $48.07 in February 2020, nearly 12 years later. Much of the world, of course, was very dependent on the Middle Eastern nations, Russia, and other oil-producing nations for their energy supply. The dependency heavily influenced geopolitical, diplomatic, and military considerations, resulting in significant armed conflict and strained global relationships. However, by the period's end, energy exploration and production capabilities had advanced sufficiently, with the help of considerable advancement in electronics technology, that fracking methods allowed the United States to achieve energy independence and lessen oil supplies as a source of global tensions.

While the legacy of Third Industrial Revolution was hanging over the 1970s and 1980s, the technology of the Fourth Industrial Revolution began to take off. Initially, led by IBM, Digital Equipment Corporation, and others, large computing systems became increasingly powerful and were used to automate basic business tasks, such as finance, human resources, and inventory management. However, with Intel's microprocessor, the personal computer became a reality with Apple and IBM at the forefront. As Nordhaus (2021) has shown, the cost of computing continued to fall rapidly.

It turned out that microprocessors also permitted advances in other computer hardware, such as servers, expanding the range of software functionality to databases, mail, printing, web services, and games. With computing costs falling and functionality growing, by the late 1980s and early 1990s, tasks were partitioned among various servers. And by the early 1990s, Intel had learned how to move its technology from generation-to-generation, using pricing to make each generation attractive to users, and profitable for Intel, while holding competitors at bay. By the late 1990s, the combined impact of the technology and the market strategy was effective enough to see measurable productivity gains in the economic statistics.[7]

---

7 Notwithstanding the technology advances of the 1990 to 2022 period, Strauss and Howe (1997) provided a prescient view of the challenges to be encountered in the generation ahead.

While Intel's success on the supply side was making semiconductor technology and its business model viable, advances in optical networking, and client–server as well as the design of the World Wide Web and the creation of the web browser made the Internet a viable platform for business activity. As would be expected in an industrial revolution, a frenzy emerged—the dot.com bubble—in which an uncountable number of businesses were launched attempting to deploy the novel technology. However, in the absence of new, innovative business models, most failed to exploit the new technology with significant financial capital destroyed. The 2001 recession and equity market collapse were required to clean up the mess.

It was not until the 2007 launch of Apple's iPhone combined with the creation of Google, Facebook, and Amazon, along with Microsoft's focus on the Internet browser, that the required technology and business models began to align. With many other entrepreneurs learning from these early, successful ventures, both e-commerce and advertising-supported services grew rapidly with mobile devices and Internet service providing a convenient and workable infrastructure. With investors seeking to protect wealth and grow income, a wide array of complex financial instruments, most notable in the housing and mortgage lending sector, were created in the first half of the 2000s decade. However, the widespread failure of such instruments and the subsequent 2008–2009 financial market crash cleansed balance sheets and prepared investors for the technology-driven growth that has followed.

While it's much too soon in the course of economic history to make a definitive declaration, the 1990s dot.com bubble and the 2008–2009 Great Recession appears to have marked the end of the Fourth Industrial Revolution's installation period and the possible beginning of the deployment period. However, the weak, disappointing, and stuttering growth during the decade between the Great Recession and the global pandemic demonstrates the difficulty in launching more rapid growth. With robust economic growth, productivity growth, and capital investment spending having failed to emerge, uncertainty remains. But the increasing adoption of the new technology, by consumers, workers, businesses, and governments, and the increasing digital intensity of economic activity generally suggests a corner might have been turned.

Four Industrial Revolutions: Parallels, But No Repetition

As the story of Charles Dickens visit to America suggests, there are parallels across each period. Harberger's "mushrooms" appear in each era's early period when a wide range of technological applications spring forth. While the legacy of the prior era hangs heavily over the early years, even decades, resistance to change is substantial and protection of income and wealth by those who were the prior eras' winners is strong. Time is required for the previous eras' capital to age and depreciate when the prior era's technology is exhausted. Failure is also necessary as entrepreneurs learn, from trial and error, and the process of creative destruction reveals which new business models will succeed.

After a global recession and financial market crash cleans up the mess that's been created, Harberger's "yeast" appears. The new technology and new business models begin to slowly take hold. But overcoming the resistance to change is critical and, as history suggests, is never easy. Creative destruction requires knowledge diffusion and the ability of lagging firms to absorb the new technology with new business models by deeply transforming their businesses. Likewise, governments and households need to transform their activities. If successful, tangible and intangible investment becomes more robust, as new capital replaces old capital. With the combined new technology and new business models, the result is massive transformation of how work gets done and lives are lived. With new capital investment, economic and productivity growth strengthens. But the issue is what causes businesses, households, and governments to take the risk and discard old ways and adopt new ones.

CHAPTER 4

Superstar Firms, Knowledge Transfer, and Labor Income Share

Industrial revolutions are characterized by investment and depreciation of tangible and intangible capital that embodies new and legacy technology whose ability to add value is dependent on creative destruction across business organizations, worker cohorts, and governments as new products and services are launched, new business models are created, and existing business processes are transformed.

In this chapter, two critical features of industrial revolutions are examined—(1) knowledge transfers and absorptive capacity and (2) changing capital and labor income shares with a shifting income distribution. Both differ fundamentally over the course of each industrial revolution and define the dynamics of systemic change. In the installation period of each industrial revolution, high productivity, leading-edge firms absorb knowledge effectively and find new applications for the new technology, resulting in market share gains, increased industry concentration, and reduced labor expense as a percent of revenue. Income is skewed toward capital owners and away from labor. The high productivity, leading-edge firms are labeled superstar firms. But the star-lit nature of the leaders implies there are laggards. This chapter considers, in detail, the laggards and the opportunities they offer for productivity improvement as productivity performance is highly variable and widely disbursed across industry firms. While the determinants of productivity are unsettled, worker engagement has received less than needed attention, especially in a services-driven economy. So, the chapter explores the contribution of workers to productivity growth and the conditions under which labor effort is automated and, conversely, where capital—principally technology capital—augments workers' efforts.

Recall that the trend in nonresidential tangible and nontangible investment growth slowed from 4 percent in 1967 to less than 2 percent in 2009 with only a short-lived bump during the 2000 dot.com bubble. Nonetheless, incomes continued to grow, most notably for those with great wealth and high incomes. Figure 4.1 shows the trend in nonresidential investment growth and the share of incomes of those in the top 1 percent as a percentage of total national income. After reaching a peak of 22 percent in the early 1940s, the income share of the top 1 percent of earners fell over the entire deployment period of the Third Industrial Revolution. As incomes grew, incomes of lower wage earners grew more rapidly than those at the top, resulting in a fall of the income share of the top 1 to 10 percent by the late 1970s. However, as growth slowed and real wages began to stagnate, the income of the top 1 percent began a 30-year march upward, continuing to 2010 and reaching 20 percent. The recent plateauing of high earners income share, if it is to be a peak, remains slightly below its previous 1920's peak.

Income and wealth protection is not limited to the last quarter of the 20th century. It's an innate human instinct. It happens that the data are now more readily available (see Appendix C). With stagnate real growth and income and wealth protection, the distribution of income has returned to proportions last realized in the 1920s and 1930s.

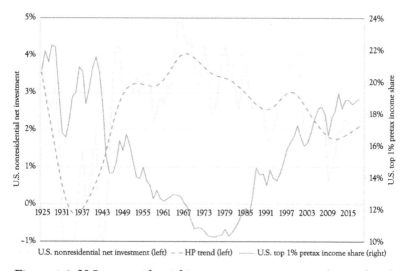

Figure 4.1 U.S. nonresidential investment as a percent of capital and U.S. top 1 percent pretax income share

Source: See Figure 2.3 and Saez and Zuckman (2020).

With legacy capital embodying the previous era's mature technology and generating high income, the capital stock begins to experience increased deprecation, which over time slows its productive capacity and value creation. Simultaneously, a new technology appears that is, initially, expensive and limited in application. As the technology develops, costs decline, applications broaden, and the promise of income-generating opportunities expand with creative destruction showing the early signs of the transformation to follow. Nonetheless, excessive optimism inflates asset values that are corrected in a protracted global financial crisis.

In the aftermath of the crisis, cleansed balance sheets and available cash are positioned to invest in the now mature and inexpensive new technology with the replacement of then-aged tangible and intangible capital. However, even more intense creative destruction produces fundamental change, establishing a new order, cutting across labor and product markets with widespread adoption of new business models, processes, products, and services. Because such deep and profound change is resisted by entrenched interests—wealth holders, business organizations, workers, and governments—often major external events such as wars, depressions, and pandemics are required to cause new social and economic regimes to emerge. However, if creative destruction and the ensuing regime transformation are successful, robust output and productivity growth are expected in a low inflation environment.

If such broad-based macroeconomic benefits are to be realized, the move through an industrial revolution requires knowledge transfer (see Coyle 2021). The early technology and business model transformation leaders—for example, Facebook, Amazon, Apple, and Google—see their experience and knowledge transferred to newly launched firms and to productivity lagging firms. The rewards that these early leaders and their workers have reaped are shared with those who follow.

Knowledge Diffusion and Absorptive Capacity

If organizations are to fully benefit from the renewal of tangible and intangible capital, an ability to absorb knowledge is critical. Industry productivity leaders, by their nature and organizational culture, understand how to learn, transform, and grow. The absorptive capacity of organizations and the rate of knowledge diffusion—"two sides of the same coin"—depend on the nature and extent of capital and labor interaction. The diffusion of knowledge only creates economic value if organizations have the ability to absorb such knowledge and create productive improvements. Indeed, successful creative destruction—launching innovation, creating new firms, and finding new job roles—requires knowledge diffusion and absorptive capacity.

Cohen and Levinthal (1990), in a classic paper, define absorptive capacity as the ability of a firm to recognize the value of new, external information, assimilate such information, and create economic value. Importantly, innovative capabilities are a function of prior related knowledge and diversity, making the absorptive capacity path dependent with investment in tangible and intangible capital necessary for future success (see also Bessen 2015).

Using cross-sectional survey data on technological opportunities and appropriability conditions, Cohen and Levinthal model firm-level investment in research and development (R&D). The dependent variable is R&D intensity, defined as company-financed business-unit R&D expenditures as a percentage of business unit sales and transfers over the period 1975 through 1977. Technological opportunity is assessed with what are considered two critical sources of such opportunity—the science base of the industry and extra-industry sources of knowledge.[1]

Cohen and Levinthal's findings point to the importance of the interaction between knowledge appropriability and the industry four-firm concentration ratio over the period of their data. Industry knowledge was more easily captured or shared when a larger proportion of industry sales were concentrated among the largest industry players. In addition, the percentage of an industry's tangible capital installed within the preceding

---

[1] The relevance of 11 basic and applied fields of science and the importance of external sources of knowledge to technological progress in a line of business are included. Intra-industry R&D spillovers are represented with six measures used by firms to capture and protect the competitive advantages. These measures include patents to prevent duplication, patents to secure royalty income, secrecy, lead time, movement down the learning curve, and complementary sales and service efforts. A subset of these measures enter the model appropriately signed and are significantly different from zero.

five years was positive and significant in the model. Industry leading firms who had recent experience growing their tangible and intangible capital were more likely to invest in new knowledge.

These findings suggest that when learning is difficult, an increase in the relevance and quantity of knowledge has a more positive effect on industry R&D intensity and absorptive capacity. Cohen and Levinthal suggest that under such circumstances, basic science is more important than applied science with targeted knowledge important in support of absorptive capacity. The importance of knowledge originating from universities exceeds that from government labs, which, in turn, is greater than that for material suppliers, which exceeds that for equipment suppliers.

As shown by Cohen and Levinthal, knowledge diffusion is required for knowledge absorption. Akcigit and Ates (2021) explore a theoretical and empirical treatment of a decline in knowledge diffusion between productivity leading and laggard firms in the 1980–2010 period. They suggest that a decline in knowledge diffusion emanating from productivity-leading firms implies higher markups and profits as well as a labor income share decrease. The dominant force is the shift to more concentrated sectors—consistent with Cohen–Levinthal findings—where more productive firms thrive with fewer workers. While the Akcigit and Ates (2021) model does not directly speak to the observed decline in the firm entry rate, the increase in market concentration implies that new entrants are likely to compete against dominant market players, which would discourage firm creation and knowledge diffusion.

Bessen and Nuvolari (2016) consider knowledge sharing from a historic perspective. They cite the work of Robert Allen as an illustration. Allen (1983) writes that the pig iron industry of Cleveland, UK, in 1850 to 1870—the deployment period of the First Industrial Revolution—observed "free exchange of information about new techniques and plant designs." The knowledge exchange encouraged innovation building on previous advances. Bessen and Nuvolari conclude that knowledge sharing was not rare or marginal. Important technologies at the center of industrialization, such as steam engines, iron and steel production, steamboats, and textile production, were developed as a result of a collective effort.

Figure 4.2 expands the Akcigit and Ates view of business establishment formation from 1980 to 2010 to 1948 to 2018. After an increasing business formation rate from 1960 to 1978, the figure shows a decline in business formation from 1980 to 2010, similar to the decline shown in Figure 7 in the research by Akcigit and Ates (2021).

The 1948–1980 period approximately coincides with the years that have been identified as the deployment period of the Third Industrial Revolution. With the fossil-fuel, mass production era having reached maturity and tangible and intangible capital in a period of rapid accumulation, including government sector infrastructure and intellectual capital, business formation began a period of rapid increase. Interestingly, more than a decade was required for the formation rate improvement to begin. By the later portion of the period, business formation accelerated to a very high rate. Once underway, the formation rate remained elevated for three decades.

By contrast, the 1980–2018 period approximately aligns with the installation period of the Fourth Industrial Revolution. With the aging capital of the previous period and the nascent technology of the new electronics and IT era, business formation slowed. As Akcigit and Ates suggest, industry concentration increased. The leadership of IBM in the computer industry and later by Intel, Corp. in the semiconductor

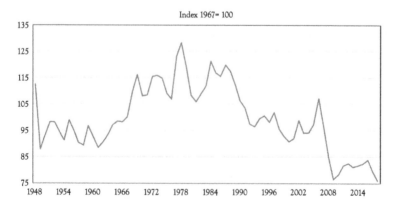

Figure 4.2 U.S. net business establishment formation rate

Source: Historic Data Colonial Times to Present, Part 2, Business Enterprise, Series V 20–30 Business Formation and Business Failures 1857 to 1970; Statistical Abstract, Various Issues, 1980–1990; and U.S. Census Bureau, 2018 Business Dynamics Statistics 1979–2018.

industry are examples of concentration in the newly formed technology industry. Eventually, of course, newly formed highly innovative industries, such as keyword search, social media, and browser software, also showed new business formation and high concentration.

Labor Income Share

Akcigit and Ates suggest that declining knowledge diffusion from productivity-leading firms results in a labor income share decrease with more productive firms thriving with fewer workers. The labor share decrease implies higher markups and profits along with a shift to more concentrated sectors.

The decline of labor's income share across the industrialized economies is, by now, well-known and well-documented.[2] As is also well-known, it was long understood that labor income was a constant share of GDP. Kaldor (1961) famously cited the stability of labor's early 20th century income share as a "stylized fact." The post-1980 fall in the U.S. labor income share, shown in Figure 4.3, has eliminated stable labor income share as a fact. Autor et al. (2020) find that labor's income share fall is "real and significant" and not a result of mismeasurement. Autor et al. also assert that the cause of the share decline is not as a result of "rapid declines in quality-adjusted equipment prices, especially of information and communication technologies," "social norms and labor market institutions, such as unions and the real value of the minimum wage" and "trade and international outsourcing."[3]

Autor et al. analyze U.S. Economic Census data for six large sectors over three decades: 1982 to 2012.[4] The covered employment makes up

---

[2] See Autor, Dorn, Katz, Patterson, and Van Reenen (2020) for an empirical review of labor shares across 12 OECD and a literature review of the fall in labor share.

[3] Autor et al. do not find manufacturing industries with greater exposure to trade shocks lose labor share relative to other manufacturing industries, but observe employment declines in such industries. They also find a decline in labor's share in nontraded sectors, such as wholesale trade, retail trade, and utilities.

[4] The six sectors are manufacturing, retail trade, wholesale trade, services, utilities and transportation, and finance.

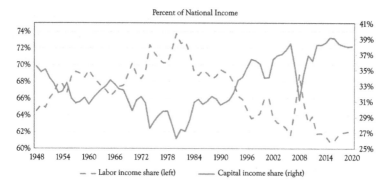

Percent of National Income

Figure 4.3 U.S. domestic income real factor income

Source: U.S. Bureau of Economic Analysis. National Income and Product Accounts. Table 1.13. National income by sector, legal form of organization, and type of income goods, rows 4, 5, 6, and 7 with author's calculations.

approximately 80 percent of U.S. employment and GDP with data for 676 industries of which 388 are in the manufacturing sector. They also draw on the 2012 release of the EU KLEMS database to measure international trends in the labor share and augment the measurement of the labor share in the U.S. Economic Census.

At the detailed industry level, Autor et al. find there has been a "rise in sales concentration … across the vast bulk of the U.S. private sector, reflecting the increased specialization of leading firms on core competencies" (p. 650). Autor et al. label the industry-leading, high-productivity firms as "superstar firms," calling to mind the current small set of well-known technology firms. However, their data cover 676 four-digit industries, suggesting that the phenomena are widespread across industry sectors.

The industries that have become more concentrated are those with faster productivity growth. Each industry's productivity-leading firms—superstar firms—are not only more innovative but also are larger firms and getting larger while realizing higher markups. As a result, those industries with increased product market concentration, more rapid productivity growth, and enhanced innovation have experienced larger declines in the labor share. Innovation combined with economies of scale has reduced labor expense as a percent of revenue. Because labor shares tend to be lower in larger firms, reallocation of market share to larger firms has tended to depress aggregate labor share.

Importantly, Autor et al. also show that the share declines are largely due to the reallocation of sales and value added between firms rather than a fall in the labor share for the average firm. The reallocation-driven fall in the labor share is most pronounced in the industries exhibiting the largest increase in sales concentration. These same patterns are also present in other OECD countries.

To the extent that the advent of new technology increases automation, lowers marginal costs, and increases markups, labor's income share rises at the firm level among productivity-leading firms. When "market toughness" increases—as defined by lower marginal cost—an aggregate labor income share decline requires between-firm reallocation—the shift of market share to more productive firms.

Finally, Autor et al. observe that a high level of concentration does not necessarily mean persistent dominance. In the spirit of creative destruction, one dominant firm could quickly replace another. If incumbents are more likely to innovate than entrants, incumbency could create advantages for firms with a high market share. Conversely, dominant but complacent firms could be replaced by more eager entrants. Rising industry concentration among productivity-leading firms is more prevalent in industries with quicker technology adoption and more rapid total factor productivity (TFP) growth. As has been experienced in the 1982–2021 period, the result is a reallocation of output toward high productivity and low labor share firms.

Shifting capital and labor income shares were also a dynamic element in the early industrial revolutions. Allen (2009) identifies "Engels' Pause" as the period that aligns with the First Industrial Revolution's installation period in which UK technology innovations revolutionized industries with Britain's income shares remaining relatively constant, as is expected in the installation period of each industrial revolution.

Acemoglu (2002) argues that technological change in the late 18th and early 19th centuries may have been biased *toward* unskilled labor. Increased demand for those unskilled workers in the new factory system was the product of the "invention of a new method of invention." Consequently, there was a large migration of unskilled workers to English cities and a large increase in population.[5] Despite the bias toward

---

[5] From Chapter 3, the parable of Charles Dickens 1842 visit to Lowell, MA and his high praise for "the mills girls" also reflected the bias toward unskilled labor in the American textile industry.

unskilled labor and the expectation that wages would rise as a result, the increased labor supply put downward pressure on wages.

Both Allen (2009) and Crafts (2021a) simulate counterfactuals that eliminate the population explosion. Both find the population shocks undermined the First Industrial Revolution's potential to raise real wages. Because labor's income share is the product of the average wage rate, labor force participation, and population, migrating workers add to the available workforce, independent of population growth. Increased participation of unskilled labor can hold labor's share constant, while the average wage rate is declining. Appendix D considers "Engels' Pause" in more detail.

While industrial revolutions are characterized by investment and depreciation in tangible and intangible capital, it is also characterized by differential knowledge diffusion and changes in labor income share. The high-productivity firms—superstar firms—with leading-edge capabilities are able to capture the early benefits of the new technology in the industrial revolution's installation period, resulting in declining labor income share as has been seen in the recent three decades. Lagging firms wait until the new technology is less expensive, well understood, and the extent and nature of the necessary creative destruction are clear in the deployment period.

As the deployment period progresses and knowledge diffusion is more readily available with increased absorptive capacity on the part of recipients, a broader cross-section of industry firms are able to (1) adopt the new technology, (2) creatively destruct their existing business models and processes, (3) innovate with lessons learned from industry leaders, and (4) profitably invest in new tangible and intangible capital. With such widespread adoption, macroeconomic benefits are likely with more rapid output and productivity growth and low inflation.

With superstar firms benefiting from innovation and strong productivity growth, the question is around the reason productivity lagging-firms lag. Profit and income opportunities are lost because of the inability to innovate, deploy technology, and transform. Presumably, there is an absence of both management and technical skill as well as the profit and income motivation to risk the attempt at transformation. However, history suggests the transformation eventually occurs. The issue for lagging firms is what are the considerations and forces that ultimately lead to the transformation and regime switching moving in the deployment era.

Persistent Productivity Differences

The existence of superstar firms as shown by Autor et al. follows a growing body of research and scholarship that has established "enormous and persistent productivity differences across producers even within naturally defined industries" (Syverson 2011). These differences are not fleeting with higher productivity firms more likely to survive over long periods (Foster, Haltiwanger, and Syverson 2008). While such persistence is often attributed to technological diffusion, the literature is quite clear that productivity differentials appear to be the result of investments in intangible capital—the business know-how embodied in capabilities across organizations.

Over the past decade, the developed-world productivity growth slowdown has been especially pronounced in the United States and the United Kingdom. Table 4.1 shows the well-recognized slowing across major regions with the sharpest falloff in the Anglo-Saxon nations. However, the aggregate-level productivity slowdown hides the slowdown even among the most productive, superstar firms and the deterioration of creative destruction and resource reallocation (Andrews, Criscuolo, and Gal 2016). As can be seen in Figure 4.4, not only is value added per worker growing more slowly in both the manufacturing and the services sector laggard firms, but growth has also slowed among the frontier firms. Even among more productive U.S. firms, Akcigit and Ates (2020) find that resource reallocation has been slowing since the 1980s with the slowdown even more striking since the 2000s.

While determinants of productivity at the firm level remain unsettled, much is known about a broad set of influences. Building on a growing body of work, Bloom, Brynjolfsson, Foster, Jarmin, Patnaik, Saporta, and Van Reenen (2019) find enormous dispersion of management practices across plants, with 40 percent of the variation across plants within the same firm. Management practices account for more than 20 percent of the productivity variation with a similar, or greater, percentage attributed to R&D, information and communications technology (ICT), or human capital. Two key drivers of improved management are right-to-work laws and learning spillovers.

Talent and human resource management, more generally, have also been shown to impact productivity. Mas (2008) shows the resale values of

Table 4.1 Developed economies labor productivity

Labor Productivity Annual Growth		
	1998–2010	2011–2017
UK	1.5%	0.3%
United States	2.3%	0.4%
EU11	1.1%	0.8%
Japan	1.2%	1.0%

Source: World KLEMS Data, Release 2019. LP1_G Growth rate of value added per hour worked, %, log.

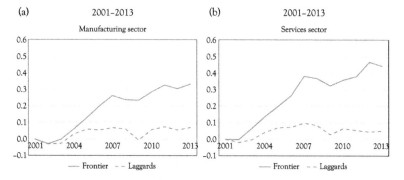

Figure 4.4 Value added per worker
Source: Andrews, Criscuolo, and Gal (2016).

equipment made at plants and times where Caterpillar was experiencing labor strife during the 1990s, compared to otherwise identical products made at plants or times without unrest, had about 5 percent lower resale values. The productivity impact due to the implied reduction in the equipment's quality-adjusted service flows totaled $400 million.

Establishing causality for the role of talent and management practices remains a difficult issue. To explore the issue, Bloom, Eifert, Mahajan, McKenzie, and Roberts (2013) conducted a randomized field experiment with management consulting provided to a random set of Indian firms. Comparing productivity growth in the treatment group to a control group not receiving consulting support, average productivity rose by 11 percent and decentralized decision making increased, as did the use of ICT.

ICT also has a role to play in gaining a productivity advantage. van Ark, O'Mahony, and Timmer (2008) show the European Union's sluggish productivity growth compared with that of the United States during the late 1990s and early 2000s can be explained in large part by the later emergence and smaller size of ICT investment across European economies. Bloom, Sadun, and Van Reenen (2012) show U.S.-based multinationals operating in the European Union are more productive than their EU counterparts with evidence pointing to a complementarity between ICT capital and human resources practices, explaining U.S. multinationals' productivity advantage in the European Union.

Brynjolfsson, McAfee, Sorell, and Zhu (2008) provide case studies where ICT enhances the speed with which firms replicate practices across lines of business. Firms that successfully innovate are able to leverage productivity advantage, quickly displace less productive competitors, and increase the volatility of the performance of all firms.

Productivity divergence and the existence of superstar firms, by implication, suggest there are productivity laggards—those at the bottom of the productivity distribution, as shown in Figure 4.4. Berlingieri, Calligaris, Criscuolo, and Verlhac (2020) explore lagging firms across 13 OECD nations—Australia, Belgium, Canada, Denmark, Finland, France, Hungary, Ireland, Italy, Norway, Portugal, Sweden, and Switzerland—with a novel data set covering the period 1995 to 2014. Lagging firms are defined as those in the bottom 40 percent in each nation's productivity distribution.

Berlingieri et al. are careful to point out that these low-productivity firms should not all be considered zombie firms. While there are some among the laggards who would typically exit a competitive market and would be considered zombies, there are also (1) SMEs who are likely to remain small and have limited scope for productivity improvement, for example dry cleaners, hair salons, fitness centers; (2) firms hit by temporary negative productivity shocks, for example extreme weather events; and (3) new entrants operating below their productivity potential in the early years of development—for example venture capital-funded firms. These bottom two-fifths, as measured by labor productivity, represent a nonnegligible 31 percent of employment, but only 12 percent of value added, and 14 percent of gross output.

Among the bottom quarter of these lagging firms (i.e., the bottom 10 percent of each nation's productivity distribution), entry and exit plays an important role. Not surprisingly, exiting firms are less productive than surviving firms, while entrants are also less productive than survivors.

With firms exiting their disappearance makes the most important positive contribution to productivity improvement among the bottom 10 percent. Among this bottom cohort, reallocation of employment and other resource to new and surviving firms matters most for productivity realization. For the remainder of the laggards (i.e., 10–40 percent of the productivity distribution), entry and exit are minor factors. The most significant contribution is from the typical surviving firm.

While productivity-lagging firms make a small contribution to productivity growth, if productivity improvement is possible, aggregate productivity gains could be substantial. A counterfactual simulation exercise by Berlingieri et al. finds remarkable potential gains from pushing the laggards to the median aggregate productivity level. Aggregate productivity would increase by 2 percent by raising the productivity of the bottom 10 percent to the median and by an even larger 6 percent if those in the 10 to 40 productivity cohorts increased to the median level. So, while resource reallocation is critical for meaningful productivity improvement, incenting and helping the typical surviving, but currently productivity lagging, firm improvement is just as important. There is tension between resource reallocation and resulting productivity improvement from firms that should exit and improvement from lagging but surviving firms. In the United States, aggregate productivity growth in the retail sector seems to be almost exclusively from new businesses, not from the improvement at surviving firms (Foster, Haltiwanger, and Krizan 2001).

Importantly, Berlingieri et al. look at the relationship between laggards' productivity growth and their distance to their industries superstar firms—the top 10 percent of the productivity distribution—which they define as the productivity gap. They find a positive relationship between the productivity gap and productivity growth of laggards, indicating that firms that are further behind realize higher productivity growth rates. Also, younger laggards catch up to the productivity leaders faster. However, the speed of catch-up has decreased over time.

Berlingieri et al. find that the laggards are catching up at a slower speed in industries using digital technologies and digital skills more intensively, as well as in industries with higher general skill levels. These weak catch-up rates suggest obstacles to the transfer of technology and knowledge might also be a cause of the increase in productivity dispersion. The digital transformation and the increased importance of knowledge appear to have raised barriers to diffusion. Laggards are lagging because they lack the necessary absorptive capacity and do not face the necessary profit and income incentives and pressures to transform. As Landes (1969) observes, among British business leaders in the First Industrial Revolution, many lagging firms appear to misunderstand that the rules of the game have changed. With both demand and supply conditions changing, the leaders of many lagging firms assume that current and past conditions will continue and fail to see the risk ahead.

Worker Contribution to Productivity Gains

With productivity divergence and the existence of superstar firms, the global productivity slowdown reflects deterioration in productivity at the sector and industry levels. As Table 4.2 shows, across the developed economies, service providers deliver 70 percent or more of value creation. Consequently, productivity improvement is highly dependent on the performance of the services sector.

Andrews, Criscuolo, and Gal (2016) use harmonized cross-country data from 24 countries to show that among the top 5 percent of services sector firms—superstar firms—in each two-digit industry, labor productivity growth between 2001 and 2013 rose at an annual rate of 3.6 percent compared to just 0.4 percent for all remaining firms—laggards. Information services firms show an even more pronounced gap between superstar firms and productivity laggards. In addition, TFP—controlling for capital deepening and mark-up behavior—shows a similar divergence, which is even more pronounced for information services firms. In the manufacturing sector, over the same period and across the same set of national economies, the superstar firms have also become relatively more productive, but at a somewhat slower rate. The manufacturing sector superstar firm productivity increased at an average annual rate of 2.8 percent compared to annual productivity gains of just 0.6 percent for lagging firms.

Heskett, Sasser, and Schlesinger (2015) summarize a substantial, four-decades body of work detailing the economics of service delivery. Leading services firms focus on factors that drive profitability, including workforce investment, the technology supporting customer-facing

Table 4.2 Developed economies services sector value added

Services Sector Value Added % of Total		
	1997	2018
UK	72.2%	79.7%
United States	74.6%	79.8%
EU11	68.8%	73.4%
Japan	64.3%	69.6%

Source: National Accounts of OECD Countries.

workers, recruiting and worker training practices, and compensation linked to performance for employees at every level.

Above-average productivity growth is achieved with high rates of repeat business that generate high-profit margins, requiring strong customer loyalty and sustained customer relationships. *The important insight is that customer loyalty is earned with high internal service quality achieved with a focus on job and workplace design, employee selection and development, employee rewards and recognition, and the technology employees utilize to serve customers.* The skill, quality, and satisfaction of the workforce, often referred to as worker engagement, is a critical element of service success. As a result, the economics of services requires innovative measurement.

While the economics of manufacturing has a much longer and more robust history with a much larger body of data in support, Betti, de Boer, and Giraud (2020) identify four recent business process transformations that 54 high-productivity manufacturing firms have successfully completed. These organizations have prioritized workforce development and engagement, transforming the nature of work through upskilling or reskilling with new ways of working.

Betti et al. find the gap between superstar manufacturing firms and others reflects four focus areas:

- Agility and customer centricity across end-to-end manufacturing and supply chains to facilitate faster recognition of customer preferences.
- Supply-chain resilience providing competitive advantage and requiring connected, reconfigurable n-tier supply ecosystems and regionalization.

- Speed and productivity attained through increased levels of automation and workforce augmentation coupled with upskilling and reskilling efforts.
- Environmental and global warming efficiency considered a requirement to remain in business and ensure compliance with an increasingly complex regulatory landscape.

A substantial literature shows the empirical link between worker engagement, customer loyalty, and profitability, especially for services sector firms (Allas and Schaninger 2020). Worker engagement is worker's involvement, satisfaction, and enthusiasm for a job role. As shown in Table 4.3, worker satisfaction also appears to contribute directly to shareholder value.

Recent research by Bellet, de Neve, and Ward (2020) exploits a natural experiment to provide evidence on the relationship between employee happiness and productivity. The happiness of British Telecom call center workers is measured over a six-month period using a novel weekly survey instrument and administrative data on workplace behaviors and measures of employee performance.

Exploiting exogenous variation in employee happiness arising from weather shocks local to each of the 11 UK call centers, including Canterbury, Turo, Swansea, Dundee, and Lancaster, a strong causal effect of worker happiness on sales is found. The effect is driven by employees working more effectively on the intensive margin by making more calls per hour, adhering more closely to their work schedule, and converting more calls into sales. No effect was found on the extensive margin on various high-frequency labor supply measures such as attendance and break-taking. Workers' weekly sales increased by 25 percent when their happiness increased by one point on a scale of one to five.

Using a regression discontinuity design, Ruffini (2020) shows that higher wages paid to low-income care-home workers increase the service quality provided to patients. A 10-percent increase in the minimum wage raises low-skilled care-home workers' earnings by 1 to 2 percent, reduces employee separations, and increases stable hires. These earnings' gains and the implied increase in firm-specific human capital translate into marked improvements in patient health and safety.

Table 4.3 Employee satisfaction and company performance, including shareholder value

Correlation between employee satisfaction and selected performance metrics[1]		Annual shareholder returns for 100 best companies to work for ("Top 100") relative to given portfolio 1998–2009[2]	
Customer satisfaction	0.31	Top 100 returns in excess of risk-free portfolio	+3.5%
Low staff turnover	0.25	Top 100 returns in excess of portfolio of similar companies	+2.1%
Profitability	0.2	Top 100 returns in excess of portfolio of companies with similar characteristics	+1.8%
Employee productivity	0.16		

[1] Meta-analysis combining observations from >1.8 million employees and 82,000 business units.
[2] Risk adjusted; based on list compiled by Fortune for the United States.

Source: Allas and Schaninger (2020).

Across the United States, the minimum wage increase for care-home workers would prevent at least 15,000 deaths, lower the number of inspection violations by 1 to 2 percent, and reduce the cost of preventable care. Firms are able to fully offset higher labor costs by attracting patients with a greater ability to pay and increasing prices for these residents, resulting in no significant change in profitability. Considering costs elsewhere in the health system, savings from pressure ulcer treatment alone offset up to half the increased wage bill. If the social value of increased longevity for care-home residents is at least $21,000—well below existing estimates— higher wages are fully offset by improvements in care.

Kaur, Mullainathan, Oh, and Schilbach (2021) show that increasing cash-on-hand among poor Indian workers raised productivity. Asserting that financial concerns led to worry and stress, interfering with the ability to work effectively, a field experiment in a piece-rate manufacturing environment was conducted. The timing of piece-rate payments was randomized such that on a given day some workers had more cash-on-hand than others. Wages and piece rates, as well as human and physical capital, were held constant.

On days on which payment is received, average productivity increased by 6.2 percent and mistakes declined, with the increase concentrated among relatively poorer workers. Faster work with fewer errors suggests improved cognition. Kaur, Mullainathan, Oh, and Schilbach (2021) assert that with the alleviation of financial concerns, workers were more attentive and productive at work.

Gilchrist, Luca, and Malhotra (2016) find higher wages elicit reciprocity and led to increased productivity. In a field experiment with data entry contract workers engaged through an online labor market platform with its largest share of workers from India, higher wages, per se, in a context of no future employment commitment, did not have a discernible effect on productivity. However, structuring a portion of the wage as a clear and unexpected gift—offering a wage increase with no additional conditions after the employee accepted the contract—did lead to higher productivity for the duration of the job. Gifts were roughly as efficient as hiring more workers.[6]

Bryl (2018) finds companies with greater human capital orientation—higher salaries and benefits, more training, a transformational leadership style, and better equipment—perform better than their peers with less human capital-orientated strategy. Among 7,204 publicly listed U.S. companies, those listed as the "100 Best Companies to Work" provided superior performance. Over 2007 to 2017, a human capital orientation strategy provided high profitability and above-average financial performance with stronger equity growth and higher market valuation.

Harter, Hayes, and Schmidt (2002) conduct a large-scale meta-analysis and find that business units with top-quartile employee engagement achieved operating-profit margins that were 1 to 4 percentage points higher than those in the bottom quartile.

Finally, consistent with the importance of worker engagement, especially in the services sector, Berlingieri, Calligaris, and Criscuolo (2018) find that wages increase with productivity in both the manufacturing and the nonfinancial market services sectors. However, the correlation between wages and productivity is much stronger in the services sector, suggesting there is a measurable productivity-wage premium in the services sector.

---

[6] Fisman and Luca (2021) cite three additional studies showing a positive relationship between wages and productivity.

Reversing Labor Income Share Decline

With technology embodied in capital investment, perhaps the most critical issue is whether capital investment and technological change substitute or complement the effort of human automation versus augmentation. Acemoglu (2002) and Acemoglu (2020) provides a framework to assess the direction of change, for example, whether technological change benefits all workers, specific worker groups, or the owners of capital. The direction and bias of changing technology are an endogenous response to expected profit opportunities.[7]

In the 1945–1975 period, the Third Industrial Revolution's deployment period, U.S. real GDP growth averaged 4 percent per year and U.S. labor productivity grew 2.6 percent per year. In the 1975–2010 period, the Fourth Industrial Revolution's installation period, real GDP grew 2.9 percent per year and labor productivity grew at 2 percent per year with little growth after 2000. With semiconductor, electronics, information, and communications technology in a nascent stage during the 1975–2010 installation period, early automation of standard business processes was found with the new technology only beginning to display signs of future potential. Business model innovation, fundamentally new management practices, and new products and services only began to appear at the end of the period (see McAfee and Brynjolfsson 2017).

The hypothesis is that as the nature of economic activity evolves from the deployment era to the installation era, regime switching occurs with labor moving from complementary to substitutability. As activity continues to evolve from the installation era to the next deployment era, regime switching occurs—again—workers' effort, which were substituted with capital equipment, are now complementary to capital equipment in the deployment period. During the installation period, diminishing services provided by an aging capital stock coincides with emerging, innovative

---

[7] The elasticity of substitution quantifies the relationship between labor's income share and the capital–labor ratio. The elasticity of substitution measures the percentage change in the capital–labor ratio compared to the percentage change in the real wage–real interest rate ratio. Appendix E presents early evidence that the elasticity of substitution changes in the movement from the installation period to the deployment period.

technology. After a disruptive major global financial crisis results in a transition of management practices and business models, the resulting regime switch impacts labor markets, just as it does other markets, resulting in moving labor from substituting to complementing capital.

Empirically, Allen (2009) identified "Engel's Pause" during the First Industrial Revolution as a period when British income shares remained relatively constant. More recently, the Third Industrial Revolution's deployment period and the Fourth Industrial Revolution's installation period saw a labor income share reversal.

Another view of regime switching from capital and labor complementary to substitutability can be seen in the study by Acemoglu and Restrepo (2019). Acemoglu and Restrepo use a task-based framework to identify where and how labor appears to complement the deployment of new technology and where automation appears to substitute for labor in the automation of tasks. Acemoglu and Restrepo write:

> New technologies not only increase the productivity of capital and labor at tasks they currently perform, but also impact the allocation of tasks to these factors of production—what we call the *task content of production*. Shifts in the task content of production can have major effects for how labor demand changes as well as for productivity.

A productivity effect results from increased value added created by automation while also displacing labor from automated tasks—a displacement effect in which labor and capital are gross substitutes. When the displacement effect exceeds the productivity effect, labor and capital are gross substitutes and labor share falls.

However, new technology can also create new tasks, expanding the tasks in which labor possesses a comparative advantage. The new tasks reinstate labor, improve productivity as new tasks exploit labor's comparative advantage, and increase labor demand. Capital and labor are gross complements.

Acemoglu and Restrepo explore the evolution of U.S. labor demand in the post-1945 era. During the 1947–1987 period, rapid growth exploiting a then-mature technology increased labor demand, complementing the deployment of capital and the wage bill per capita growing by 2.5 percent per year.[8] While on balance, changes in the task content of production were nearly zero percent, there was substantial displacement and reinstatement. Between 1947 and 1987, the displacement effect reduced labor demand by about 0.48 percent per year, while the reinstatement effect increased labor demand by 0.47 percent per year. As predicted in a deployment period, automation proceeded at pace and the introduction of new technology was accompanied by widespread task transformation, counterbalancing the adverse labor demand consequences of automation.

In the 1987–2017 period, the per capita wage bill grew by 1.33 percent per year over the period with little growth after 2000. The 1.2 percentage point slowdown in wage bill growth is in part accounted for by slower productivity growth that fell to 1.54 percent per year.

Slower wage bill growth resulted from a significant negative shift in the task content of production against labor. The change in task content was driven by an acceleration of displacing labor, reducing labor demand by 0.70 percent per year compared to 0.48 percent in the 1947–1987 period and a deceleration in the introduction of technologies reinstating labor, increasing labor demand only by 0.35 percent per year compared to 0.47 percent in the 1947–1987 period. Together, changes in the task content of production reduced labor demand by 10 percent over the period.

The shift from substitutability to complementary capital and labor, alongside the shift from automation to augmentation, impacts income distribution as shown in Figures 4.1 and 4.3. While automation occurs continuously, when conditions are ripe in the deployment period, increased aggregate demand, new task creation, and labor augmentation can reverse rising income inequality.

---

[8] The wage bill is divided by population, removing population growth as a confounding influence.

CHAPTER 5

Resource Transformation as Growth Recovers

At the dawn of the Fourth Industrial Revolution, IBM, Digital Equipment Corporation (DEC) and a small number of other large companies led the information technology (IT) industry. DEC's CEO Kenneth Olson was widely considered one of the industry's leading innovators with his technology prowess, management savvy, and organizational imagination. Twenty years earlier, as a newly minted MIT graduate, working at the university's Lincoln Lab, Olson received a number of patents for an improved version of magnetic core memory, the predecessor of the microprocessor. Core memory had been invented by Jay Forrester, then the lab's director, and Olson's long-term mentor. Very soon thereafter, an ambitious Olson launched DEC as one of the first venture-funded computer industry firms.

After two decades of success, as the Fourth Industrial Revolution began in 1977, Olson, referring to computers used in the home, was quoted as saying: "There is no reason for any individual to have a computer in his home." Olsen later said his words were taken out of context and he was referring to computers set up to control homes, not PCs. Now, four-and-a-half decades later, whatever the intent of Olson's statement, both prognostications were clearly incorrect. Homes, today, are nearly completely controlled by computing devices along with PCs, tablets, and mobile phones apparent everywhere.

At the advent of the Fourth Industrial Revolution, it was difficult for anyone, independent of his or her brilliance, to foresee the computing power we all carry in our purses and pockets today. Not surprisingly, the IT industry has been filled with what are, in retrospect, foolish predictions. Three-and-a-half decades before Olson's forecast, Thomas Watson, then-president of IBM, in 1943, said: "I think there is a world market for maybe five computers." In 1995, Robert Metcalfe, the founder of 3Com said: "I predict the Internet will soon go spectacularly supernova and in 1996 catastrophically collapse." And in 2004, Bill Gates, founder of Microsoft, said: "Two years from now, spam will be solved" (www.pcworld.com/article/532605/worst_tech_predictions.html/amp).

If the Fourth Industrial Revolution's deployment period is set to begin, it's hardly surprising that far more pedestrian business leaders in small, medium, and larger organizations are challenged to make the technology bets necessary to exploit the new digital technology. Consequently, it's also not surprising that adoption of the most advanced technology that is available today, is in the very early stages of adoption.

This chapter will focus on the transformation ahead for the tangible and intangible assets necessary for improved economic and productivity growth. Economists focus on the needed resources on the right side of the production function. Deployment of the new digital technology will increase but only in response to widespread change. The dynamics of change and transformation is explored in this chapter.

As the gap between the desired and actual capital stock widens, the previous era's embodied, but now antiquated, GPT will become insufficient. The new general-purpose technology will achieve maturity and deliver low cost. As pressure builds for creative destruction, a new period of economic, social, and political activity will appear.[1] However, robust growth is not guaranteed. If successfully innovated and deployed, new management practices and business models, supported by social and political transformation, will deliver an extended period of rapid income growth and wealth creation. As history has demonstrated, achieving a path of sustained above-average growth requires, not only an alignment of current and future financial asset values—delivered by a deep global recession and a major financial crisis—but also sufficient pressure to reduce investor, household, and business resistance. While there are few data points, the U.S. civil war of the 1860s, the global recession of the

---

[1] See Gordon (2016) and Mokyr (1998) for a discussion of social and economic transformation. For a broader discussion of social and economic transformation, see: Acemoglu and Robinson (2012) and Acemoglu and Robinson (2019).

1930s, the Second World War of the early 1940s, and—perhaps—the 2020–2021 global pandemic might qualify as having massively disrupted social and economic activity at a point in time when the global economy was prepared to enter a new era. Ironically, to realize the benefits of stronger economic and productivity growth with more equally distributed incomes, a difficult—even painful—social, economic, and political transformation must be negotiated.

Understanding what the coming deployment period—2022 and beyond—might look like requires a view of the rate and pace of change to IT, capital investment, labor markets, business strategy, and public policy.

Advanced Digital Technology Takes Hold

The semiconductor and electronics technology launched by Intel and others in the early 1970s has given rise to an inexpensive, low cost, GPT that is now in wide use across virtually every economic and geographic sector. While the digital technology that has emerged from 50 years of innovation has not only automated many previously manual business and personal tasks, it has also resulted in near-instant global communication and ubiquitous digital services, increasing personal and business efficiency. If digital technology permits the widespread use of artificial intelligence (AI) technology, the period ahead is likely to see even more significant gains (See Crafts 2021b).

In an assessment of the deployment of AI technology, Bresnhan (2019) finds leading applications in early diffusion but on a similar track as other information and communication technology (ICT) systems of the past 25 years. AI technology applications have been deployed across a range of industries but have gained most traction in consumer-oriented mass-market production, distribution, and marketing with a small set of well-known providers building a range of services on the World Wide Web with the benefit of smart phones and tablets.

Bresnahan writes that AI technologies are:

> … tools that permit the design of new productive systems. They are embedded in the capital of those productive systems. In that

regard, the AITs [AI technologies] used here are like earlier ICTs. They combine technical progress, tools for invention of applications, and technical progress embedded in capital. (Besnahan 2019, 23)

Bresnahan further observes that there is no role for task-level substitution (TLS). Rather, entirely new systems are being created in which labor and capital work in complementary fashion. The pace at which such systems are deployed in new production processes, Bresnahan writes:

depends on the pace at which whole new production processes and business models are invented (Amazon's store and mall were invented and have been constantly improved). System-level substitution depends on the competition between old and new firms, and on the effectiveness of old firms at inventing competitive responses (e.g., in Walmart inventing e-commerce services). In short, system-level substitution entails a wide variety of opportunities and barriers to invention, involves competition, and involves the development of complementary markets and services. It is the opposite of local and simple—and of TLS. (Bresnahan 2019, 24)

Bresnahan suggests deployment is in an early stage. Consumer-oriented mass-market production, distribution, and marketing systems in search, social media, streaming, and retail have achieved scale with the success of Google, Facebook, Netflix, and Amazon. However, user interface capabilities based in natural language processing, cloud computing, statistical prediction, and complementary network technology remain limited. While early success has been achieved with financial services, human resource systems, and decision support, other industry applications remain nascent.

Acemoglu, Autor, Hazell, and Restrepo (2021) find no discernible relationship between AI exposure and employment or wage growth at the occupation or industry level, implying that AI has not yet achieved detectable aggregate labor market consequences. Using detailed establishment level occupation data on job vacancies, Acemoglu et al. find rapid growth in AI-related vacancies over the 2010–2018 period. The rapid growth is not limited to the business services and IT sectors. Rather, the growth is significantly greater in AI-exposed establishments where workers engage in tasks that are compatible with current AI capabilities. Establishment-level estimates suggest that AI-exposed establishments are reducing hiring in non-AI positions as they expand AI data science-related hiring. However, the aggregate impact remains limited.

Eichengreen (2015) distinguish between the "range of applicability" and "range of adaptation." The range of applicability is the number of different sectors or activities where innovations are applied. Crafts (2002) finds early in the First Industrial Revolution that the application of the steam engine was limited to the textile industry and railways, limiting its impact on output and productivity growth. The range of adaptation refers the extent to which activity must be reorganized—transformed—before positive impacts on output and productivity growth are realized. In addition, the greater the required range of adaptation, the higher the likelihood that growth may slow in the short run, as costly investments in adaptation are sunk and existing technological complementarities are disrupted.

Similarly, Brynjolfsson, Rock, and Syverson (2021) find that as firms adopt new technology, productivity growth initially languishes. Intangible capital is necessary for business process, product, and service innovation. Later, productivity growth strengthens as capital service flows from the previously applied intangible stocks and measurable output is generated. Measured productivity growth follows a J-curve shape, initially dipping while the investment in intangible capital is larger than the investment rate in other types of capital, then rising as growing intangible stocks begin to contribute to measured production. In the long run, as tangible and intangible investments reach their steady-state growth rates, the return-adjusted value of the intangible capital services flow approach the value of the initial investment.

Zolas, Kroff, Brynjolfsson, McElheran, Beede, Buffington, Goldschlag, Foster, and Dinlersoz (2020) have undertaken, possibly, the most extensive survey of AI technology usage. They found that in 2017, across AI-related technologies, for all firms in the U.S. economy the aggregate adoption rate was 6.6 percent.[2] Zolas et al. introduced a survey module that com-

---

[2] The aggregate adoption rate is measured across five potential technologies that incorporate elements of AI—Automated Guided Vehicles, Machine Learning, Machine Vision, Natural Language Processing, and Voice Recognition—and is employment-weighted by industry sector.

plemented and expanded research on the causes and consequences of advanced technology adoption. The 2018 Annual Business Survey (ABS), conducted by the U.S. Census Bureau in partnership with the National Science Foundation, provided a comprehensive view of advanced technology diffusion among U.S. firms. The technologies included were AI, cloud computing, and the digitization of business information. The survey was a large, nationally representative sample of over 570,000 responding firms covering all private, nonfarm sectors of the economy.

First, despite widespread discussion of AI and its various applications—machine learning, robotics, automated vehicles, natural language processing, machine vision, voice recognition and other advanced technologies—Zolas et al. found the 2017 adoption rates were relatively low. Respondents were also asked about both the use and testing of the various technologies. Perhaps, not surprisingly, the highest use and testing rates were observed for the touchscreen and kiosk technology with a 6.1 percent adoption rate and less than 1 percent testing rate. Machine learning was the second most used technology with a use rate of 2.9 percent and a 0.7 percent testing rate. Voice recognition and machine vision, which are examples of machine learning applications, have the next two highest use and testing rates.

Adoption was also skewed, with heaviest concentration among a small subset of older and larger firms. The smallest firms had the lowest use rates. Even among firms of the same age, the usage rates tended to increase with size. For small firms (less than 50 employees) use rates tended to decline with age with the oldest small firms having the lowest adoption rates. Presumably, new, young born-on-the-web firms are heavy AI users. For larger firms (50+ employees), usage rates exhibited the opposite pattern. As firm age increased, usage rate also increased. The highest usage rates were in the largest and oldest firms. Overall, size was an important predictor of AI technology use and the connection between age and the use of these technologies depended on size. Scale appeared to be important for AI usage, likely due to requirements for large quantities of data, copious computing power, experienced software developers, and skilled data scientists fully exploiting AI capabilities. As might be expected, the older, larger firms, perhaps superstar firms, had a technology advantage.

Second, Zolas et al. also found that technology adoption exhibits a hierarchical pattern, with the most-sophisticated technologies adopted most often only when more-basic applications were as well. For instance, digitization of business information was very widely adopted. The vast majority of firms who utilize the cloud for their IT services also digitize their information. Similarly, the vast majority of firms that adopt at least one AI technology, almost always purchase cloud services.

Third, cloud services adoption displayed modest adoption, with a large share of firms hosting at least one IT function in the cloud. But cloud usage was significantly lower than the adoption rates of digital information storage, which is nearly universal. Cloud users overwhelmingly also displayed a higher level of digitization. Intensive use of the cloud—as opposed to limited experimentation—was slightly lower but still quite prevalent. For cloud users, cloud technology was widespread across applications, as nearly a third of each IT function was performed in the cloud with intensive usage. Like digitization, the largest firms are the most likely to adopt some cloud computing services. The relationship between cloud use and firm age is more nuanced but, typically, the lowest adoption rates are among the oldest firms.

Firms that rely on cloud computing have shifted their cost structure with increased variable cost and flexible resource management for variable, seasonal demand. The cloud infrastructure also provides the abundant computing power needed for AI applications with massive quantities of digital information.

As Zolas et al. observe, until recently, the required computing power for large-scale AI applications was beyond the reach of most firms. Cloud computing made scalable computing resources available on-demand, fundamentally changing the economics of IT. Cloud computing brings data together with storage, computing, and user interface in one location, allowing frequent updates. Importantly, with nearly ubiquitous digitized information, data management is an ongoing challenge that the cloud infrastructure helps to address.

Finally, Zolas, et al. found a positive association between technology adoption and product and process innovation. They found a great deal of diversification across technology types, with certain technologies having stronger and more positive associations with innovation than others.

As would be expected in the early years of the Fourth Industrial Revolution's deployment period, widespread use of the AI technology is in the early stages. In the early years of a possible 30-year journey, applications remain limited, a challenge to deploy, and immature. Capabilities will likely grow, expand, and simplify, leading to broad and deep adoption.

Capital Investment Recovers

With the deployment of the new technology in an early stage, the turn-around in the long-term trend in nonresidential capital investment spending is also in an early stage (see Figure 2.3). Recall that investment in tangible capital is important for a number of reasons. Tangible capital embodies new technology, with new intellectual property and significantly increased digital content, drawing on the fruits of recent research and development activity. The new advanced technology replaces the legacy technology in the depreciated capital. The creation, manufacturing, and deployment of new tangible capital is income and job creating. Depending on location considerations, new tangible capital investment could alter the geographic distribution of economic activity, aiding those areas economic activity has abandoned. With growth remaining weak, the decades-long capital investment slowdown continues to receive the attention of scholars.

Crouzet and Eberly (2020), who have published the most detailed econometric work, show the investment gap as the difference between average Q and marginal q for tangible capital. "q" is the ratio of a tangible asset's market value and its replacement value. In the post 1980s period, the investment gap can be decomposed into (1) a term capturing rents—excess profits—to physical capital, (2) a term capturing the value of intangible capital, and (3) a term capturing rents to intangible capital. The third term shows "rising rents and rising intangibles cannot be meaningfully analyzed in separation, as their interaction contributes to the gap between investment and returns" (Crouzet and Eberly 2020, 2). In simple terms, highly compensated, skilled workers contribute mightily to the return generated from capital investment.

Depending on the definition of intangibles, the rents paid to intangible assets—most often skilled works—accounts for one-third to one-half of the investment gap. With lower estimates of the increase in total rents, "user costs of intangibles are elevated, and have remained so, in contrast with the post-1980 decline in the user costs of physical [tangible] capital" (Crouzet and Eberly 2020, 2). When Crouzet and Eberly expand the definition of intangibles beyond R&D to include organizational capital, innovation, and transformation, the combined contribution of growth in the intangible capital stock and rents generated by intangible capital increases to about two-thirds.

With substantial heterogeneity across sectors, Crouzet and Eberly warn statements about the aggregate investment gap may be misleading. However, a redistribution of rewards away from capital owners and to high-wage workers—the providers of intangible capital—could be a contributing factor to weak investment spending growth.

Crouzet's and Eberly's work suggests the growth of investment has become much more dependent on the availability of a skilled workforce and somewhat less dependent on the cost of physical capital. Weak capital investment and the delayed onset of the Fourth Industrial Revolution's deployment period has also received attention under the banner of secular stagnation, a notion originally offered by Hansen (1939) and offered again recently by Summers (2014).

In reaction to the pandemic, differential tangible and intangible capital investment has resulted in a digitization divide between U.S. and European Union (EU) firms, with U.S. firms adding digital capabilities at a faster pace. Not surprisingly, the differential pace has had an effect on employment. Recent research by the European Investment Bank found that 46 percent of EU firms responded to the pandemic by becoming more digital, while 58 percent of U.S. firms have hastened their digital transformation (see European Investment Bank 2022). Among EU firms, 34 percent used the pandemic as an opportunity to start their digitalization journey. However, progress has been slow. The uptake of at least one digital technology did not progress in 2020 and 2021, remaining constant at around 61 percent of EU firms. The share of U.S. firms that have already adopted at least one digital technology is 66 percent, five percentage points higher than in the EU.

The growing digital divide also poses risks for the labor market. In Europe, 33 percent of employment is with firms that are doing nothing in the digital sphere, compared with 20 percent in the United States. These "sleepwalking firms"—as the European Investment Bank has named such firms—are also likely to pay lower wages and are less likely to create new jobs. During the pandemic, they were also less likely to train their workers.

The recent investment spending by productivity leaders highlights the response of investment spending decisions to new technology as opposed to inexpensive credit. Rachel and Summers (2019) write that a decade of weak growth and low inflation, notwithstanding inflated central bank balance sheets and rapidly rising government debt, has led to the revival of interest in the secular stagnation hypothesis, characterized by a chronic tendency of insufficient private investment, absent extraordinary policies to bring about extremely low interest rates.[3] Summers suggests:

> It is useful at the outset to consider the possibility that changes in the structure of the economy have led to a significant shift in the natural balance between savings and investment, causing a decline in the equilibrium or normal real rate of interest that is associated with full employment. (Summers 2014, 69)

Summers (2014), Rachel and Summers (2019), and Furman and Summers (2020) argue that the tendency to secular stagnation, but for extraordinary fiscal policy actions, require real interest rates "far below their current slightly negative level." Summers and Rachel estimate that the "private sector neutral real interest rate" might have declined by 700 basis points since the 1970s. But, of course, real interest rates have not declined by 700 basis points and capital investment has remained weak. Secular stagnation, as formulated by Summers with a focus on real interest rates, is further suggestive of the diminishing role of the cost of capital incenting investment spending growth.

---

[3] More precisely, Summers (2022) defined secular stagnation as "chronic excess savings that have not been fully absorbed by investment resulting in very low real interest rates best addressed by a range of measures to reduce inequality and, in particular, to promote high social return though not necessarily high private return." Famously, Bernanke (2005) observed the savings–investment imbalance with a focus on the "global saving glut."

Worker Engagement, Compensation, and Productivity

As structural forces appear to be shifting away from a traditional reliance on the cost of capital and to a reliance on the skill of the workforce, new policy issues arise. Among many scholars, Summers (2014) and Rachel and Summers (2019) advocate the need for more aggressive federal government investment. Mazzucato (2021) "looks at the grand challenges facing us in a radically new way, arguing that we must rethink the capacities and role of government within the economy and society, and above all recover a sense of public purpose."

Aggressive fiscal spending actions in response to the 2020–2021 pandemic may be providing growth benefits well beyond the period of the immediate pandemic crisis. In addition, energy technology addressing the challenge of climate change and global warming also remains in the early stages of the transition from a fossil-fuel-based technology to renewable technology. By historic standards, growth and productivity improvement remains weak, interest rates remain near zero with real interest rates negative, and inflation, until 2021, remained below the policy targets of the major central banks. As a result, questions persist around the slow pace of transformation, the events, or pressures necessary for accelerated transformation, and policy actions that might promote stronger growth.

Among many scholars, Summers (2014) and Rachel and Summers (2019) advocate the need for more aggressive federal government investment. The recent weakness in such investment is shown in Figures 5.1 and 5.2. Conversely, it is of interest to see in the deployment period of the Third Industrial Revolution the strength of federal government investment spending, preceding the rapid and robust expansion of private nonresidential capital. In particular, federal spending expanded rapidly, building the stock of intellectual property. While U.S. federal investment in intellectual property was encouraged by U.S.–Soviet strategic competition, boosting military expenditures and creating the desire to explore space, private benefits emerged. The nonrival and nonexclusive nature of public sector intangible asset investment provided private sector organizations with opportunities for growth and innovation. Similarly, the significant investment in structures—roads, bridges, and so on— also encouraged private sector expansion. More than 60 years later, the

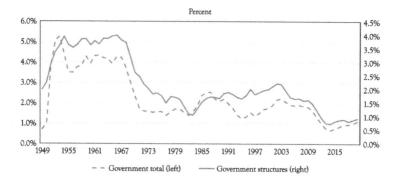

Figure 5.1 Net additions to government sector nonresidential capital stock—total and structures

Source: U.S. Bureau of Economic Analysis. Fixed Assets Accounts Table. Table 1.1 Current-cost net stock of fixed assets and consumer durable goods, row 16 and 19, Table 1.3 Current-cost depreciation of fixed assets and consumer durable goods, row 16 and 19, and Table 1.5 Investment in fixed assets and consumer durable goods, row 16 and 19.

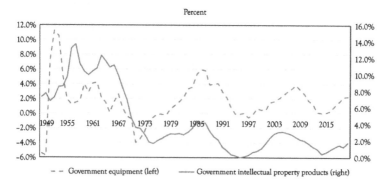

Figure 5.2 Net additions to government sector nonresidential capital stock—equipment and intellectual property products

Source: U.S. Bureau of Economic Analysis. Fixed Assets Accounts Table. Table 1.1 Current-cost net stock of fixed assets and consumer durable goods, row 17 and 18, Table 1.3 Current-cost depreciation of fixed assets and consumer durable goods, row 17 and 18, and Table 1.5 Investment in fixed assets and consumer durable goods, row 17 and 18.

infrastructure provided by such investment has depreciated significantly and lacks the electronic capability that the Internet-of-things now provides. Recently enacted infrastructure spending programs, in the United States and elsewhere, might help, along with pandemic-related aid, to support the needed transformation.

Beyond the need for a shift in the drivers of tangible and intangible capital investment, the wage structure, the work structure, and worker engagement are among the issues at the heart of the transformation. Jorgenson in a long series of papers has pointed to the importance of the quality of the labor force in productivity improvement (see Jorgenson, Ho, and Samuels 2019 for the most recent work). Workforce quality includes educational attainment, health, and well-being (See Bryson 2017). In addition, employer–employee relationships also make important contributions to productivity differences across manufacturers and service providers (see Abowd, Kramarz, and Margolis 1999). As shown in Chapter 4, a small but growing literature employs natural experiments to suggest a causal relationship between worker engagement and productivity improvement.

Worker engagement—worker's involvement, satisfaction, and enthusiasm for a job role—is gaining a growing recognition as important for productivity growth, business success, and improved living standards. Recent research finds shifts in the responsiveness of workers, across differing generational cohorts, to changes in wages (see Hotchkiss 2022). In making labor force participation decisions, compared to baby boomers of the same age, millennials are only about three-quarters as responsive to wage changes. In addition, those in the Gen X cohort are only about half as responsive to wage changes in making participation decisions, compared to baby boomers. The implication is that employers will likely have to resort to nonwage incentives to entice workers to fill open jobs, suggesting a growing focus on worker engagement.

Perhaps the most radical restructuring of worker relationships—early in the deployment period of the Third Industrial Revolution—was the 1950 Treaty of Detroit. At a time when manufacturing employment was nearly a third of U.S. payroll employment—it is currently less than 10 percent—automobile industry leaders, United Auto Worker (UAW) leaders, and President Harry Truman codified and extended institutions for labor relations that had begun in the 1930s and had been enlarged in the very different environment of the Second World War (Levy and Temlin 2007).

In an initial 1948 contract negotiation round, General Motors (GM) proposal to the UAW included an increase in wages, a cost-of-living adjustment, and a 2 percent annual improvement factor, which would increase wages every year in an attempt to allow workers to benefit from productivity gains. The UAW, in exchange, would allow management control over production and investment decisions, surrendering job assignment seniority and the right to protest reassignments.

For the next two years, workers realized wage increases and gains from productivity. GM enjoyed smooth, increasing production, and established a net income record for a U.S. corporation in 1949. When the contract period ended, the UAW and GM readily agreed to a similar plan that was extended to include a pension plan and a health insurance program.

Importantly, the successful auto industry agreements soon scaled to other industries. Wages in a group of heavy industries moved virtually identically because of the economic, political, and institutional interdependence among the companies and the unions in these industries. Wages in industries outside this group were largely determined by spillover effects of the key group wages as well as economic variables applicable to the industry. Agreements to create pension plans ultimately spread to other industries, including the rubber industry, Bethlehem Steel, and then U.S. Steel. As is well known, these work arrangements continued into the 1970s and were correlated with the period of strong productivity growth that followed, which eventually began to slow in 1973.

While the Treaty of Detroit is an illustration of a radical institutional change, the deployment period of the Third Industrial Revolution also brought substantial change in the U.S. federal minimum wage, providing an additional data point of substantial, institutional change.

Between 1950 and 1979, there were 12 statutory U.S. federal minimum wage increases, or an increase approximately once every two-and-a-half years. However, in the Fourth Industrial Revolution installation period, from 1980 to 2020, there were eight such increases, or an increase every five years, on average. The current federal minimum wage is $7.25 where it has stood since July 2009. As shown in Figure 5.3, measured in real terms, the U.S. federal minimum wage reached a peak in 1968 and in 2020, the wage is at 60 percent of its peak.

While the federal minimum wage is not dispositive in establishing the wage structure, it is indicative of the extent to which real wages have declined, especially at the low end of the wage structure. With such a decline, it would be reasonable to hypothesize that for workers at the low end of the wage distribution, engagement is less than it might have been in the past.

Figure 5.3 U.S. federal minimum wage

Source: Federal Reserve Bank of St. Louis, FRED Economic Data.

The real minimum wage of the major European nations has also experienced stagnation in the recent period. Figure 5.4 shows after substantial improvement of the inflation-adjusted minimum wage prior to the 2008–2009 global financial crisis, the real wage has fallen since 2008. After a falloff, the real wage now lies 3.6 percent below its 2008 peak. Nonetheless, the real minimum wage of the major European nations has trended up over the period since 1999, while the real minimum wage in the United States has trended down.

Indeed, Dustmann, Lindner, Schönberg, Umkehrer, and vom Berge (2020) investigate the wage, employment, and reallocation effects of the introduction of a nationwide minimum wage in Germany, affecting 15 percent of the labor force. Exploiting variation in exposure across individuals and regions, Dustmann et al. find that the minimum wage introduction raised wages, but did not lower employment.

However, Dustmann et al. also find the wage change did lead to reallocative effects. Low-wage workers, but not high-wage workers, were induced to move from small, low-paying firms to larger, higher paying firms, accounting for up to 25 percent of the overall increase in daily wages low-wage workers experienced following the minimum wage introduction. In addition, average firm productivity increased in more affected regions in the years following the introduction of the minimum wage.

In the United States, recent work by Stansbury and Summers (2020) cites declining worker power as a unified explanation for rising profitability

2012 dollars, 1999: Q1=100

— France, Spain, Germany, and UK   - - - U.S.

Figure 5.4 Real minimum wage index

Source: Monthly minimum wages for France, Spain, Germany, UK and U.S. Quarterly data 1999 to 2021. German minimum wage instituted in 2015. Index is GDP weighted. Sources: Nation Minimum Wage data from countryeconomy.com; France, Germany, and Spain CPI and GDP data from Eurostat; UK and U.S. CPI and GDP data from Federal Reserve Bank of St. Louis, FRED Economic Data.

and market valuations of U.S. businesses, sluggish wage growth, and reduced unemployment and inflation, especially in the recovery from the 2008–2009 financial crisis.

Beyond issues related to the *wage* structure, one might also expect changes in *work* structure, such as outsourcing or off-shoring, to impact employer-employee relationships. Goldschmidt and Schmieder (2017) conduct an event study in Germany to show that wages in outsourced jobs fell by 10 to 15 percent relative to similar jobs not outsourced. Wage losses associated with outsourcing stem from a loss of firm-specific rents, suggesting that labor cost savings are an important reason firms choose to contract out services. Goldschmidt and Schmieder tie the increase in outsourcing to broader changes in the German wage structure, in particular showing that outsourcing of cleaning, security, and logistics services alone account for 9 percent of increased German wage inequality since the 1980s.

While wages and compensation are important, the hypothesis is that it is the broader dimensions of the employer–employee relationship— worker engagement—that contribute to or detract from persistent productivity differences across manufacturers and service providers. The worker engagement hypothesis not only asserts the existence of current differences but also the assertation of persistence. The hypothesis follows from the ability of superstar firms with highly engaged workers to successfully transform activities in response to changing market conditions and customer demands.

In the process of creative destruction, workers also bring pressure to bear. In transforming their behavior, adjusting their compensation expectations, and revising their career projections, pressure builds for transformation. Mokyr (1998) and others have documented the selectivity bias among the skilled and able workers who are willing to relocate and seek new opportunities. Similarly, Yellen (1984) hypothesized that productivity improvements can be realized as higher real wages influence workers in a variety of ways, such as reduced turnover. Conversely, an "adverse selection" mechanism can result in the lowest-quality workers agreeing to work for less, with diminished productivity.

Wages, compensation, skill development, career advancement, work environment, management relationships, all contribute to worker engagement and, thus, productivity. Further, the issue is to understand the extent to which improvements in worker engagement can scale to provide broader economywide benefit. The improvement of income and private sector social welfare benefits along with an improved management and decision-making framework, captured in the Treaty of Detroit and subsequently scaled across the U.S. economy, appear to have been correlated with subsequent productivity improvement at the macroeconomic level.

Finally, business strategy undoubtedly also faces the need to transform in fundamental ways. The Fourth Industrial Revolution's installation period—like those preceding it—focused on invention and innovation at the level of basic systems and electronics. In the current deployment period, invention and innovation will be at the system level. The installation period is a time of experimentation for business models as well as for the technology. As the technology matures, as engineering successfully embeds the technology in the capital investment, and as successful business models are discovered, the installation period can give way to the deployment period. After the assets that funded poor investments are washed out in the major financial markets crash, new, often revolutionary business models begin to appear. As Bresnahan observes, Amazon would be Exhibit A of a radical new business models and processes, building on revolutionary new technology, with a fundamentally new business model.

CHAPTER 6

Conclusion

Is a Growth Revolution Possible?

The deployment era of the Fourth Industrial Revolution is not assured to deliver robust and rapid growth, capital deepening, and improved living standards. Clearly, the future is uncertain. A breakthrough is not guaranteed. The concern is well founded. Both in the United States and Europe, periods following economic shocks have often experienced limited growth. In the United States, between 2007 and 2020 after the Great Recession and financial crisis, U.S. real GDP growth averaged only 1.3 percent per year.

The slowdown is often referred to as hysteresis—the persistence of negative effects after the initial cause is removed (Summers 2014). Blanchard, Cerutti, and Summers (2014) examine 122 recessions over 50 years in 23 countries, finding a high proportion has been followed by lower output or slow growth. Blanchard and Summers (1986) argue that economic shocks have a persistent effect on unemployment. Citing 15 years of steadily rising European unemployment, they distinguish between insiders and outsiders in wage bargaining. If wages are largely set by bargaining between insiders and firms, outsiders are disenfranchised and wages are set with a view to insuring the jobs of insiders. Membership considerations, and lack of fundamental transformation, can explain the tendency of the equilibrium unemployment rate to follow the actual unemployment rate.

Consequently, if robust and rapid growth is forthcoming, it is likely that economic, social, and political transformation is required. Public investment in both tangible and intangible capital is certainly a requirement. Policy actions that encourage the deployment of the new technology along with those that support and promote both the engagement of workers and the development of skills for newly required tasks is also necessary. More fundamentally, it is the resistance to change that must be overcome if workers, business leaders, public officials, and capital owners are to risk setting aside old, comfortable ways to adopt new and different ways. The hope of improved and more equal living standards, as income and wealth accumulate, calls for new ways of working, leading, and investing. Posen (2021) writes, "the United States needs to embrace economic change rather that nostalgia."

The 2020–2021 Global Pandemic

As Landes and Lazonick observed, the success of each industrial revolution depends, in part, on the interest and ability of workers and businesses to transform behavior and engage in creative destruction. For example, as the Second Industrial Revolution moved from installation to deployment, American, German, and Swiss firms moved rapidly to adopt the new technology and make the needed capital investments, while British business leaders and workers guarded the status quo, living off existing income-producing capital. Similarly, the UK, Germany, and U.S. transformation from the installation period to the deployment period of the Third Industrial Revolution, as Landes and Gordon observed, was in part a result of the shock to economic activity in support of the war effort; an unwillingness to return to old, prewar ways; the economic rescue after the war; and substantial infrastructure spending as part of the strategic competition with the Soviet Union. Now, if the global economy, especially the developed world, is to move into the deployment phase of the Fourth Industrial Revolution, the shock and dislocation of the 1990s dot-com bubble and the 2008–2009 Great Recession and financial crisis appears to have been insufficient to create the needed pressure for change. However, much as the conclusion of the Second World War appears to have created circumstances for the Third Industrial Revolution's deployment period, perhaps the combined effect of the Great Recession and the 2020–2021 pandemic will create conditions for the Fourth Industrial Revolution's deployment period.

The pandemic's disruption and devastation could possibly prove severe enough that not only will workers feel compelled to fundamentally alter their behavior but so will governments, businesses, and households. Perhaps the old prepandemic ways are gone. The 2020–2021 pandemic arrived following 40 years of creation, innovation, and deployment of ICT. As digital technology matured and became inexpensive and ubiquitous, it's possible that a period of robust growth could lie ahead. While automation has replaced some tasks that some workers have performed, world-class technology combined with transformation in how business is done offers the possibility that new tasks are being created with a new period of robust growth ahead.

Among the many surprises that the COVID-19 pandemic has brought, is the reluctance of some workers to return to prepandemic jobs. After the initial spread of the virus and a brief two-month recession, employment quickly rebounded, and unemployment began to fall. However, for an extended period in 2020 and 2022, workers were reluctant to fully engage. At 62.2 percent in mid-2022, those in the United States working or looking for work, as a percent of the working-age population, remained at a depressed level not seen in four and a half decades. The participation rate decline represents a loss of nearly four million workers.

As is well known, in 2021, workers were quitting their jobs at a very high rate. Late in the year, 4.5 million U.S. workers per month were quitting, 3 percent of those employed. Both the number of quits and the quit rate were at record highs. The phenomenon has been called The Great Resignation. At the same time, both the number of job openings and the job opening rate were also at record highs. While it's too soon to know the definitive cause of the extremely elevated quit rate, the resignations were heavily centered in service industries where workers have little flexibility but to engage with patients, clients, and customers daily. With the pandemic creating meaningful risk with such interaction, it is hardly surprising that workers in health care, retail, food service, and accommodations were quitting at high rates.

In addition, the manufacturing sector has been victimized by the largest percent increase in quits with a 58 percent increase from prepandemic to late 2021. Quits in the nondurable goods sector rose 68 percent while quits in the durable goods sector rose 52 percent. Other industries, while experiencing a larger number of quits, had a much smaller percent increase (see Long 2022).[1]

While the pandemic is an opportunity for workers to reconsider career options in light of the dislocation and transformation the pandemic might bring, similarly, business leaders might also seek to transform their workforce with high job opening rates. In late 2021, U.S. job opening rates were high in transportation and warehousing as well as professional and business services, along with industries with high quit rates—health care, retail, food service, and accommodations.

In a recent survey by Adobe, 35 percent of enterprise workers said they plan to switch jobs in the next year. However, an even larger proportion of workers earlier in their careers are seeking such changes. Among millennials 49 percent are open to a job change, while 56 percent of those on the Gen-Z cohort said they plan to pursue a new job in the next year. As shown in Table 6.1, these generations are also the least satisfied with work–life balance with 78 percent of millennials and 74 percent of those in the Gen-Z generation searching for improved balance. These cohorts are also looking for more work-schedule control and the option to work remotely.[2]

One of the many social experiments the 2020–2021 pandemic drove was a massive shift to working from home (WFH). In a multiwave survey of 30,000 Americans, Barrero, Bloom, and Davis find that 20 percent of workdays will be supplied from home after the pandemic ends, compared with just 5 percent pre-2020. The increased frequency of WFH in the

---

[1] While all the quitting and job switching was occurring, an increased number of older workers were also retiring. Faria-e-Castro (2021) finds that in 2020 and 2021 a significant number were workers who may have retired as a result of perceived health dangers as the pandemic progressed. With data through August 2021, Faria-e-Castro finds that slightly over 2.4 million excess retirements were, perhaps, due to the pandemic. The excess retirements were more than half of the 4.2 million workers who left the labor force from the beginning of the pandemic to the second quarter of 2021.

[2] In another recent survey, PWC (2021) found that 65 percent of employees are looking for a new job and 88 percent of executives are seeing higher turnover than normal.

Table 6.1 Gen-Z and millennial job switching

	Likelihood to Switch Jobs in the Next Year	Switch Jobs for Better Work–Life Balance	More Control Over My Work Schedule	The Option to Work Remotely
Gen-Z	56%	74%	66%	63%
Millennial	49%	78%	73%	66%
Gen-X	31%	66%	59%	53%
Boomer +	18%	50%	46%	37%

Source: Adobe (2021).

https://blog.adobe.com/en/publish/2021/08/26/new-research-from-adobe-document-cloud-shows-how-pandemic-is-changing-our-relationship-with-time

www.adobe.com/pdf-page.html?pdfTarget=aHR0cHM6Ly93d3cuYWRvYmUuY29tL2NvbnRlbnQvZ GFtL2R4LWRjL3VzL2VuL3BkZnMvL3RoZS1mdXR1cmUtb2YtdGltZS5wZGY=

period ahead is a result of the better-than-expected experience during the pandemic, a greatly diminished stigma associated with WFH, and lingering concerns about crowds and contagion risks. In addition, investments in computing capabilities, communications resources, and home office space make WFH viable over the long term.

Barrero, Bloom, and Davis also suggest three consequences of the increased inclination of WFH. First, workers will enjoy large benefits from greater remote work, especially those with higher earnings. Second, the shift to WFH will directly reduce spending in major city centers by at least 5 to 10 percent relative to the prepandemic situation. Third, employer plans and the relative productivity of WFH imply, according to Barrero, Bloom, and Davis, a 5 percent productivity boost in the post-pandemic period due to reoptimized working arrangements. However, only one-fifth of the productivity gain will show up in conventional productivity measures, because they do not capture the time savings from less commuting.

Speculation abounds about workers' concerns. Generous unemployment benefits, fear of SARS-CoV-2 infection, child care and elder care responsibilities, and a search for new career opportunities are among the expected causes. The constant presence of the virus along with the dreadful and deadly impact of the disease has raised fear and anxiety with continuous worry about an uncertain outcome. U.S. Census Bureau data suggest that while those suffering from depression and anxiety had diminished at the end of 2021, 41 percent of U.S. adults continued to suffer from anxiety to some degree and 38 percent from depression.

Another measure of worker stress is the extraordinarily high proportion of savings. In line with generous U.S. government stimulus payments, precautionary saving exploded. Personal saving as a percentage of disposable personal income reached a record high 33.7 percent in April 2020. After some decline, the saving rate returned to 5.4 percent in mid-2022. A portion of the saving, of course, resulted from a lack of opportunity to spend during the pandemic. Some workers saved some or all of government stimulus payments. But the jump in the April 2020 saving rate to four times its long-term average was quite striking.

Humans have reacted very differently to the pandemic. Some are in denial, others have unfortunately resorted to excessive use of drugs or alcohol, and still others to violence. Of course, many have accepted the science and adopted recommendations for the use of masks, social distancing, and vaccination. With an unseen virus and the unknown disease impact, the social psychology of pandemics has influenced a range of social behavior—from crime to auto accidents—to economic activity—personal saving, spending, workforce participation, ways of working, shopping, and digital technology adoption.

These psychological effects appear to have carried over to the labor market. With workers' continuing concerns over infection and vaccination as well as responsibilities at home, many workers appeared to have reacted to the pandemic's pressures by reassessing their careers, job opportunities, income-earning potential, and prospects. While some workers were reassessing their career choices, others were finding new directions. Among the pandemic's anomalous labor market phenomena, was a substantial surge in applications for new businesses. Over 2020 and 2021, the pace of new business formation was the highest on record from data extending back to 2004. The large increase was for new businesses that have both new employees as well as those without employees.

In contrast to the sharp and persistent decline in new business formation during and after the 2008–2009 Great Recession, the 2020 to 2021 surge in new business applications was concentrated in a few sectors—e-commerce; professional, scientific, and technical services; and accommodation and food services. With retail, accommodations, and food services having suffered especially large declines during the pandemic, the patterns were consistent with pandemic-induced labor market restructuring (Haltiwanger 2021).

Perhaps surprisingly, the current pandemic's emerging behavior pattern appears to be consistent with those of the past. With 700 years of UK data, recent scholarship has found across 19 previous pandemics over the last millennium, the aftermath has brought depressed real interest rates, rising real wages, and stronger real GDP per capita growth. Tangible and intangible capital are destroyed in wars but not in pandemics. Instead, pandemics appear to induce labor scarcity and a shift to precautionary savings—much as today.

Careful scholarly attention to the 14th century's Black Death pandemic, for example, has found that events such as the Peasants' Rebellion in England feature centrally in a narrative of rising worker power, an emergence of labor scarcity, rising real wages, and a decline in the rate of return on land. While the Black Death is a distant event and a pandemic of extreme scale, the finding is consistent with statistical evidence of the aftereffects of all 19 previous pandemics (Jordà, Singh, and Taylor 2020).

Pandemics are similar to a randomized control trial on a larger scale with microbiology providing the natural assignment mechanism. Pandemics are nonmilitary events with 100,000 or more deaths and episodes with large labor force contractions that increase the capital/labor ratio. Capital is destroyed in wars, but not in pandemics. Pandemics induce relative labor scarcity and a shift to greater precautionary savings. The relative abundance of capital suggests a response of the real natural rate of interest and a countervailing response in real wages.

Some examples of what the future might look like are already available. The miraculous vaccine advances delivered by the pharmaceutical industry is an example of the surprising advances that are likely to be repeated. Likewise, the willingness of governments to adopt new agile approval processes to rapidly bring vaccines to the global population represent a transformation that is unlikely to be forgotten by government professionals. The newfound focus on the effects of climate change, the automotive industry's commitment to electric vehicles, and the need to modernize the national electric grid are all examples of radical transformation that create jobs, build incomes, and support a fundamentally new way of life.

The psychology of pandemics has very likely altered long-term behavior. With the 2020–2021 pandemic coming as it has when the developed world appears to be entering a period of improved and sustained long-term growth, the resulting pandemic-driven dislocation could increase the pressure for increased digital intensity across a much larger universe of firms and industries that have lagged in technology innovation and adoption.

Actions Required for Improved Growth

The 2020–2021 global pandemic has clearly disrupted businesses, households, and governments. With many families experiencing devastating consequences and many businesses destroyed, the open issue is whether the shock has been of such size as to create sufficient pressure to drive fundamental change—overcoming the hysteresis effect. Increased use of e-commerce and work-from-home are changes of the nature that were in train well before the pandemic. It's possible that the pandemic's disruption and devastation has been severe enough that governments, businesses, and households will not return to old prepandemic ways, but will transform to new ways. As Aghion, Antonin, and Bunel (2021) write, such is the power of creative destruction.

Such radical transformations have been experienced in the past. The military build-up for World War II resulted in a large number of young men—there were also a number of brave young women—gaining new skills, military discipline, and experience that, at the conclusion of the conflict, were applied to business and government with new education opportunities. Workers, often women, on the home front similarly gained new labor market experience. The manufacturing sector had converted almost completely to war-time production. At the conclusion of the war, the manufacturing sector, largely, did not return to late 19th-century technology, but deployed the then-mature 20th-century technology. While the 2020–2021 pandemic has inflicted disease and death on the scale of a world war, it remains to be seen how businesses, households, and governments transform in the aftermath.

In the years ahead, the outcome will, ultimately, depend on the nature of the social contract that emerges among workers, business and political leaders, and owners of capital. Economic shocks do not, by their nature, deliver negative outcomes. The direction of the impact depends on the response of the social and economic system. With sufficient leadership, flexibility, and foresight, transformation can deliver a positive future. To achieve that future, there are a number of actions to be taken and events to occur.

As we have written at length, economic shocks have played an important role in each industrial revolution. Each has had a global financial crisis intervene. In the two most recent revolutions, the Second World War and the 2020–2021 pandemic occurred following a financial crisis as the deployment period was set to begin. While we have argued that each global financial crisis was to a great extent an endogenous shock—originating from within the economic system—the Second World War and the 2020–2021 pandemic are largely exogenous shocks—principally caused by forces outside the economic system. Similarly, while we have argued that innovation as well as tangible and intangible capital investment are an endogenous response to perceived income and profit opportunities, the technology that prevails in each industrial revolution—steam engine, electric power, semiconductor technology—is to some extent exogenous, as other options were generally available.

However, in the presence of such shocks, cultural traits matter. The interest and ability of successive generations of business leaders and workers in learning and adapting to a changing environment plays a critical role in determining not only whether there is a regime switch from an installation period to a deployment period but also the rate and pace at which such a transformation occurs.

Joel Mokyr attributes the onset of the industrial era in western Europe, in part, to the greater willingness of generations of European to place less importance on traditional ways of thinking in the presence of technology and economic shocks. On the contrary, in the Chinese culture, where history played a vital role, traditional ways were maintained for an extended period (see Mokyr 2018). Nathan Nunn has developed a "theory behind cultural evolution and the empirical evidence supporting its ability to explain" economic history. Nunn provides, from an evolutionary perspective, "insights into a range of phenomena within economics, including a deeper understanding of human capital, innovation, ... [and]

the effects of market competition." The theory helps in the understanding of why persistence and path dependence are observed, and, "why sustained economic growth is often so elusive" (see Nunn 2021).

Nunn argues, culture is efficient and when "traditions are passed down over generations, individuals are able to effortlessly make decisions in complex environments" where determining "optimal action with certainty is costly or even impossible … Culture allows societies to accumulate an evolved body of knowledge that is greater than any single individual could learn within their lifetime."

However, the efficiency of culture and its traditions depend on the stability of the economic environment and the cost of acquiring new—nontraditional—knowledge and information. As the probability of an economic shock increases, lower learning costs make nontraditional actions less costly. When the state of the world changes, for example when a new, inexpensive technology becomes ubiquitous and tangible capital is highly depreciated, traditional practices are mismatched with optimal actions. The mismatch can generate disagreement and polarization among those with deeply held values and beliefs. The severity of the mismatch depends on the extent of environmental instability and the cost of individual verification. The industrial revolution framework, developed in this book, can help reduce the verification cost by providing a view of where economies are in the context of long-term growth variation.

Despite often deep differences in culture, values, and beliefs, the European Investment Bank (2022) has found that the pandemic has prompted many firms to accelerate their transformation. Indeed, the bank found that firms that lack climate action are also those with a weak capacity to transform more generally. "Wait-and-see" firms—as the bank calls them—are less likely to innovate, have success in export markets, or employ advanced management practices. These firms are also less likely to be profitable and slightly more likely to face financial constraints. The bank finds that climate risk awareness, perception, and information help determine whether firms pursue climate investments (European Investment Bank 2022, 8).

Notwithstanding the success of those frontier firms that have transformed aggressively, if global warming is to be limited to below 2°C and achieve net zero emissions of carbon dioxide and other greenhouse gases from human activities in the second half of the 21st century, energy transformation must accelerate. Much is needed to achieve these long-run goals with little consensus on the path forward. Fries (2021) finds there is broad agreement in economics on using (1) emissions pricing to internalize the environmental externalities and (2) government policy support for research and development. Among lagging firms, if emission pricing is ever successfully implemented, the cost of emission will stand in contrast to the falling price of renewable energy. However, both emission pricing and falling renewable energy prices have yet to be deployed at scale. In addition, as Fries observes, there is little current agreement on the use of other policy instruments, such as market-creating and industry-supporting policies. Nonetheless, in prior industrial revolutions, such policy actions have been used to advance energy system transformations.

A second important area for policy action is worker training and skill development. As we have observed, pandemics do not destroy tangible and intangible capital; however, they have caused labor forces to contract. Hershbein and Holzer (2021) find that while caseloads per se do not have much impact on employment, economic restrictions and mortality rates do. While the effects of economic restrictions fade once they are eased, the effects of past mortality rates accumulate and, as we have seen, workers are resigning and quitting to reassess future employment options. Beyond the impact of the pandemic, as we have discussed, workers are facing a new technology, creative destruction, and transformation. The result will be the creation of new tasks with new skill requirements.

Holzer (2019) has developed a lengthy agenda to support the development of worker skills, support education, and incent labor supply growth.

- Reforms in Social Security and Medicare that encourage longer working lives and later retirements;
- Immigration reforms that raise current levels of immigration while shifting its relative emphasis from family unification to skills and labor market needs;
- Improve the ability of U.S. students, especially those who are disadvantaged and first-generation college enrollees, to obtain postsecondary credentials;

- Expand student attainment of "21st Century Skills" that will likely make them more complementary with and less substitutable by new automation;
- Create systems of "lifelong learning" in which workers who have experienced, or are at risk of, technological displacement can more easily obtain new skills that complement automation in the workplace;
- "Make Work Pay" with the use of the earned income tax credit (EITC) to improve work incentives while raising net incomes for low-skill or displaced workers;
- Address barriers to participation, such as opioid addictions and criminal records; and
- Provide more access for lower-wage workers to paid family leave.

Changing culture and tradition is never easy. Values and deeply held beliefs are retained by many based on views, opinions, and practices passed down through many generations. However, if costs are high enough and dislocation is great enough, values and beliefs can and do change. Government policies and programs can help but are likely to be insufficient.

The Growth and Transformation of the Business Sector

As we wrote at the outset, this book's purpose is to examine the economic logic of the variation in long-term growth. With an exploration of four industrial revolutions, it's apparent that it is innovation and creative destruction, occurring in the context of cultural change that encourages nontraditional approaches on the part of both business leaders and workers. It is that change that is eventually embodied in tangible and intangible capital investment and that powers the economics of long-term growth variation. The economics, in turn, is driven by the diffusion and absorption of the innovation and transformation that emerges from the ensuing creative destruction, setting aside traditional practices. While superstar firms at the productivity frontier quickly realize the gains from innovation and creative destruction, those firms lagging in their adjustment and productivity improvement need to have the incentive and opportunity to act. In Harberger's "yeasty" metaphor, as innovation and creative destruction expand, the leavening and growth of economic activity is reenforced with increased capital investment—capital deepening—creating virtuous growth—a positive feedback loop.

As we learned earlier, over the long run, Caballero (2010) estimated the process of creative destruction accounts for over 50 percent of productivity growth. In addition, Berlingieri et al. (2020) showed that among the bottom 10 percent of productive firms, those exiting make the most important positive contribution to productivity growth. In the period ahead, the rise in bankruptcies resulting from the 2020–2021 pandemic could help to speed the exit process. Entrants, as they are on the path to achieving scale, are less productive than survivors. Among the bottom 10 percent cohort, reallocation of employment and other resources to new and surviving firms matters most for productivity realization. For the remainder of the laggards—10 to 40 percent of the productivity distribution—the most important contribution is from the surviving firms.

While productivity lagging firms make a small contribution to productivity growth, if productivity improvement is possible, aggregate productivity gains could be substantial. Berlingieri et al. found remarkable potential gains from pushing the laggards to the median aggregate productivity level. Aggregate productivity would increase by 2 percent by raising the productivity of the bottom 10 percent to the median and by an even larger 6 percent if those in the 10 to 40 percent productivity cohort increased to the median level. So, while resource reallocation is critical for meaningful productivity improvement, incenting and helping surviving but lagging firms improve is just as important as encouraging entrants and exits.

In the period ahead, encouraging new firms with available capital and, as appropriate with government support, along with incenting and helping surviving firms are critical growth elements. The expectation is that digital intensity of surviving firms will increase. It's possible that the desire to increase digital intensity among productivity lagging firms has increased as a result of the pandemic's experience. While e-commerce and work-from-home capabilities have increased, they are likely just early examples of where digital intensity is headed. Zolas et al. (2020) found that in 2017, across AI-related technologies, for U.S. firms the aggregate adoption rate was 6.6 percent. Unpublished estimates provided by a global technology provider found 4 percent of global large enterprises were operating AI solutions in 2016, 5 percent were operating such solutions in 2018, and 9 percent in 2020. The new ICT and AI technology will continue to experience cost declines and will also continue to improve its ease of use. As the technology is adopted for new applications, new sources of value will be created, new tasks required, and new capital investment needed. All will contribute to stronger growth.

As we saw in the Second Industrial Revolution, nonsuperstar firms with lagging innovation, diminished competitiveness, and lack of technological intensity suffered from deeply rooted cultural barriers that are not easily overcome. The status quo was jealously guarded. Transformation requires not only an expansive view of future profit and income opportunities but also an understanding of (1) how the competitive landscape is changing and (2) the required set of strategic priorities (see Acemuglo 2002). With some help, success is possible. As we saw earlier, the randomized field experiment with management consulting, conducted by Bloom et al. (2012), found an average productivity increase of 11 percent in the treatment group compared to the control group with increases in decentralized decision making and the increased use of ICT. It's difficult to find government-sponsored programs that have provided similar results.

In the First Industrial Revolution, Landes (1969) details business leader's strong resistance. Only the strongest incentives persuaded entrepreneurs to accept change. Entrepreneurs discovered that, with rising demand, marginal costs were rising as well. The inadequacy of the legacy technology created pressure for improvement. Entrepreneurs learned that the reduction in cost resulting from the new technology would sufficiently cover the expense of the needed investment in the new capital and technology. Despite the powerful business case for growth and expansion, entrepreneur's resistance stemmed from a new and unknown risk environment.

In the Second Industrial Revolution, the rapid industrial expansion of a unified Germany grew from a recognition of the new innovative and competitive landscape included global competition, the power of corporate enterprises, research and development of new productive resources, the interaction of organization and technology, the required human resources, and the commitment of financial resources. German entrepreneurs were trained in the new science and technology, worked hard, and were astute financial managers.

While government programs and policies can support the needed regime switch from the installation to the deployment, more is necessary. Business leader—most notably those in productivity lagging firms—must (1) feel sufficient pressure to transform, (2) correctly perceive future income and profit opportunities, (3) possess and/or acquire the skills necessary to lead the transformation, and (4) believe the emerging ICT and AI technology is on a path for low cost and productive application.

Improved Worker Engagement

While government programs and policies, depending on their design and implementation, can and will likely impact growth, each industrial revolution has shown that the interest and ability of workers and firms to adapt and transform is just as important. The extent to which culture allows for the meaningful development of nontraditional job roles and tasks—created by employers and accepted by employees—stronger growth in the deployment period is likely to emerge. As we showed in Chapter 4, there is a growing body of evidence suggesting that increased worker engagement—worker's involvement, career path assessment, compensation, satisfaction, and enthusiasm for a job role—has a positive effect on productivity. However, engagement is highly dependent on the trust between employers and employees.

Brown, Gray, McHardy, and Taylor (2015) found a positive relationship between measures of workplace performance and employee trust (see Appendix F). For example, restricting paid overtime potentially erodes employee trust, while requiring employees to take unpaid leave appears to have no effect on employee trust. Nevertheless, business leaders face a challenge. Job or work reorganization, growing out of transformation and creative destruction, is associated with lower employee trust experienced at both the employee and organizational level. In any transformation effort, worker training, education, support, and incentive compensation are all important tools to smooth the implementation of the needed changes. In a hopeful note, Brown et al. present evidence that the introduction of new technology with adequate worker compensation can result in successful change.

Like business leaders, workers make forecasts of future income opportunities. While workers are unlikely to provide themselves with spreadsheet detail and precision, workers understand the trade-offs implied by the choices they face. In the First Industrial Revolution, we saw the factory system meant a separation of work from the means of production. The worker no longer had to be both entrepreneur and worker. The worker could leave the pressures of building and managing a business to someone else. The trade-off was that the factory system imposed a new form of discipline under the watchful eye of the factory overseer.

In the Third Industrial Revolution, the 1950 Treaty of Detroit brought together automobile industry leaders, United Auto Worker (UAW) leaders, and President Harry Truman to codify and extend a structure for labor relations that had begun in the 1930s and had been enlarged in the Second World War (Levy and Temlin 2007). In an initial 1948 contract negotiation round, General Motors (GM) proposal to the UAW included an increase in wages, a cost-of-living adjustment, and a 2 percent annual improvement factor, which would increase wages every year allowing workers to benefit from productivity gains. The UAW, in exchange, allowed management control over production and investment decisions, surrendering job assignment seniority and the right to protest reassignments. For the next two years, workers realized wage increases and gains from productivity. GM enjoyed smooth, increasing production, and established a net income record for a U.S. corporation in 1949. When the contract period ended, the UAW and GM readily agreed to a similar plan that was extended to include a pension plan and a health insurance program.

The Treaty of Detroit is an illustration, not only of effective institutional change but also an employer–employee arrangement in which labor and capital were complementary and consistent with recent scholarship. Acemoglu and Restrepo (2019) show rapid growth in the 1947–1987 period—the deployment period of the Third Industrial Revolution— exploited a then-mature technology, increasing labor demand, complementing the deployment of capital with the wage bill per capita growing at 2.5 percent per year. As predicted in a deployment period, automation proceeded at pace and the introduction of new technology was accompanied by the widespread task transformation, but the consequences of automation were counterbalanced by strong aggregate demand growth and 2.4 percent average annual productivity growth.

However, in the installation period of the Fourth Industrial Revolution, 1987 to 2017, Acemoglu and Restrepo (2019) show, the per capita wage bill grew at 1.3 percent per year over the period with little growth after 2000. The 1.2 percentage point wage bill growth slowdown is in part accounted for by slower productivity growth, which fell to 1.5 percent per year and, in part, from a significant negative shift in the task content of production against labor. The change in task content was driven by (1) an acceleration of labor displacing technology, reducing labor demand by 0.7 percent per year compared to 0.5 percent reduction in 1947 to 1987 and (2) a deceleration in the introduction of technologies reinstating labor, increasing labor demand only by 0.3 percent per year compared to 0.5 percent in the 1947–1987 period. Together, changes in the task content of production reduced labor demand by 10 percent over the period.

Fiscal, Tax, and Monetary Policy

Across the developed world, a wide range of policy actions have been pursued over the last five decades. Some more successful than others. Despite the wide range of policy actions—higher taxes, lower taxes, more spending, less spending, easy monetary policy, and tight monetary policy—growth and capital investment have been disappointingly impervious to alternative policy regimes.

Over six decades, tax incentives for tangible and intangible investment have been in place more or less continuously. Periodically, these incentives have been strengthening. The 1980s focus on supply-side economics resulted in the very comprehensive 1986 reform of the U.S. tax code, while the 2000s brought a series of Bush administration business and personal tax reductions as did the late 2010s with Trump administration's tax law changes. The result is a U.S. tax on returns to tangible capital investment, currently estimated to be approximately 5 percent. Interestingly though, the current U.S. tax on returns to intangible capital—the investment in human resource—is estimated to be 28.5 percent (see

Acemoglu, Manera, and Restrepo 2020). Notwithstanding the favorable treatment of tangible capital, the rate and pace of investment continues to lag. However, to the extent that intangible assets have taken on a larger role in recent decades, a better-balanced tax policy could prove beneficial. Nonetheless, ultralow tax rates have had seemingly little impact on desired macroeconomic outcomes.

Beyond tax policy, a variety of spending measures have either been proposed or enacted by many nations, again with some but limited effectiveness. Undoubtedly, government support for education, training, and skill development has proven to deliver benefits across many nations. However, in the United States, spending on worker training, in particular, has lagged that of other nations. Similarly, U.S. infrastructure spending for both physical infrastructure—roads, bridges, ports, water supplies, and sewer systems—as well as virtual infrastructure—Internet service coverage—has also lagged but is likewise regarded as necessary in support of growth. The recent infrastructure commitment by the U.S. congress and the Biden administration is an important and long-sought step. However, it will be years before the initiative bears fruit in terms of stronger macroeconomic growth. In addition, for the most recent 20 years, U.S. military spending—which often funds research and development activity as well as other activities in support of civilian sector growth—has continued to expand rapidly. Again, like tax policy, questions abound regarding the efficacy of such policy efforts.

While capital availability has generally not been an issue in recent decades, budget policies that seek to balance budgets, bringing together tax and spending policy, can also impact capital investment decisions. However, in the United States, despite an inability to balance budgets, capital has continued to flow and lack of available capital has not been a cause of disappointing growth.

Over the long term, financing current government operations from current revenue while funding long-term commitments, such as infrastructure spending, with borrowed funds is desirable. Nonetheless, in the United States, the last year in which federal revenue was more than spending was 1999. The surplus was achieved after nearly a decade of effort by the congress and the Clinton administration attempting to enact a balanced budget. After the productivity surge of the mid-1990s and a series of tax increases, by 2001, the prospect was for a series of budget surpluses. In fact, Alan Greenspan, then Federal Reserve Board Chair, speculated that not only would deficits disappear but so would U.S. government debt. In mid-2001, Greenspan said: "current forecasts suggest that under a reasonably wide variety of possible tax and spending policies, the resulting surpluses will allow the Treasury debt held by the public to be paid off" (Greenspan 2001). Of course, the fear of eliminating Treasury debt and a disappearance of the Treasury market was unfounded, as a series of tax reductions enacted in the early 2000s as well as the impact of the 2008–2009 Great Recession caused U.S. federal debt to balloon again.

More recently, generous spending programs to ameliorate the impact of the 2020–2021 pandemic on businesses and households has resulted in a very substantial debt increase. In addition, the demographics driving the retirement surge now underway will most certainly result in still further substantial debt increases. Despite very reasonable concerns that debt levels in the United States and elsewhere will be excessive in the decades ahead, capital availability has not been a limiting factor. In the case of the United States, Treasury securities continue to hold great appeal, especially to foreign investors. Periodic concerns about excessive debt crowding out private investment and resulting in punishingly high interest rates have been unfounded. With abundant funds flowing into the U.S. Treasury, interest rates have remained very low—near zero for over two decades—a series of U.S. presidential administrations and congresses have continued spending growth without the need for tax increases.

Just as U.S. debt and deficit policy has proven not to be a capital constraint, Federal Reserve monetary policy has likewise not been a constraint. Indeed, monetary policy has been very growth supportive. For 20 years, monetary policy has provided abundant liquidity at near-zero interest rates. In late 2002, Alan Greenspan raised the specter of deflation, saying "recent experience understandably has stimulated policymakers worldwide to refocus on deflation and its consequences" (Greenspan 2002). Deflation—a fall in the general price level as opposed to slower increases—is a much-feared phenomenon. As prices fall, businesses and consumers expect continued price declines resulting in the postponement of spending, raising the possibility of declining economic activity and, in the extreme case, depression. With prices, as well as eventually wages, falling debt repayment becomes a serious problem. In the intervening 20 years, since Greenspan's initial warning, abundant liquidity, easy monetary policy, and near-zero interest rates has been the response to a series of policy challenges—the 2008–2009 Great Recession and financial crisis, the 2011–2013 eurozone recession, and the 2020–2021 global pandemic.

Despite abundant and inexpensive capital, generally low marginal capital tax rates, and continued spending growth, economic and productivity growth has continued to lag with historically slow tangible and intangible capital investment spending. Very likely, there is no silver bullet. After nearly 50 years of effort from policy makers and political leaders across the developed nations and from all political points of view, there has, thus far, been no single set of policy initiatives that has been effective in solving the problem of slow growth and skewed income distribution.

The notion of the existence of a silver bullet—highly accurate and effective—is frequently applied to a problem that has been difficult, complex, and hard to resolve.[3] While selective policy actions taken by the developed nations over recent decades have provided value, collectively, economic and productivity growth have remained disappointing.

The Growth Revolution Ahead

For the United States, United Kingdom, and other developed nations, benefit from a period of stronger economic and productivity growth with a more equal distribution of incomes will require a new social contract among workers, business leaders, and government officials, both elected and appointed.[4] Tradition and culture are important, but the willingness of productivity-lagging but surviving businesses to embrace lower-cost technology that will continue to be easier to deploy will be necessary. Likewise,

---

[3] Sir Walter Scott may have been the first to use the idea of a literal silver bullet in *Lockhart* published in 1808. The term gained appeal in the first half of the 20th century when the popular western hero of the radio and television program, *The Lone Ranger,* used a silver bullet. The phrase is almost always used in a statement that no solution exists (https://idioms.thefreedictionary.com/silver+bullet).

[4] Credit to Jim Spohrer for introducing the notion of a new social contract. Also see Shafik (2021), Shafik (2018), and Manyika, Madgavkar, Tacke, Woetzel, Smit, and Abdulaal (2020).

a substantial proportion of the workforce will also need to be willing to transform job roles and take on new tasks. Government leaders will need to show a willingness to comprise and adapt to the new economic environment. It is unlikely there is a single government policy or program that will be the silver bullet, delivering achievement of stronger economic and productivity growth with a more equal distribution of incomes.

A new social contract is required. Whether implicit or explicit social contracts govern the functioning of economies and societies. Without specifying all elements of such a contact, the expectation is that workers, business leaders, and government officials will all contribute to the transformation and needed creative destruction in the years ahead. Workers should realize all jobs will change. Occupation change generally takes decades to occur, but tasks and job roles change frequently. Workers are reluctant to change and transform, but with adequate, business-provided training, support, education, and incentive compensation, workers are willing to adopt new approaches. Government training and education programs can be beneficial as well.

Similarly, business leaders must come to recognize that future income and profit will be driven by the transformation and creative destruction growing out of the declining cost and increasing ease of use of AI technology along with investment in tangible and intangible capital. In the years ahead, it is increasingly likely that competitive pressures and shifting economics will force firms, hoping to survive, into meaningful change. Workers will need to be willing to join in the transformation process. Governments will want to incent change and support the development of the needed resource.

Importantly, political leaders will need to be willing to compromise. While common ground is unlikely, reasonable give and take will be necessary for progress. The United States, for example, is the only developed nation requiring a super majority for meaningful legislative enactment. Whether or not the U.S. Senate revises its parliamentary rules, compromise is necessary for progress.

While government programs and policy actions are and can be very beneficial, to realize the benefits of the regime switch from a move into the deployment period of the Fourth Industrial Revolution, deep cultural change is required, improving the balance between traditional and nontraditional values, beliefs, and practices. Here is a growth and fairness agenda to promote and encourage the transformation necessary for more robust income and productivity growth with more equal income distribution that deserve the attention of business and political leaders as well as workers.

Table 6.2 Growth and fairness agenda

Traditional Policy Insufficient	• No silver bullet; many policy options tried • Capital investment depends on intangible assets, less dependent on cost of capital • Aged capital embodies legacy technology
Promote Confidence Among SMEs	• Productivity gains among leading edge firms • Large number of SMEs with limited data science skill • Ease of use will increase advanced digital technology
Encourage Improvement and Fairness in AI	• Advanced digital technology deployment limited • Data becomes more available, businesses transform • Ethics and fairness take on new importance
Support Deeper Worker Engagement	• Workers respond to career, less to wage increases • Services sector dominates economic activity • Workers increase willingness to transform
Seek New Social Contract	• Businesses and workers overcome change resistance • Nostalgia for earlier eras set aside • Tolerance for diverse views increases

- **Recognize traditional policy actions may be insufficient to achieve stronger long-term growth**

  Across the developed world, a wide range of policy actions have been taken over the most recent four decades. Despite the wide range of actions taken, economic and productivity growth remains disappointing. While appropriate policy actions are important, consistency is also important.

  Perhaps, more importantly, the recent challenge of faltering democratic processes, and the possibility of increased autocratic rule, across the developed nations has raised concerns that are likely to be a more serious impediment to growth than is inconsistent or ineffective fiscal, tax, or monetary policy. The inability of political leaders to take actions in the general interest of their constituents is sufficient to prevent policy-led improvements in economic and productivity growth. Consistent leadership matters. Among the strongest performing developed economies over the past decade and a half has been Germany. The continuous strong leadership of Prime Minister Angela Merkel has undoubtedly contributed to the growth performance. Conversely, the extended debate in Great Britain over the exit from the European Union has increased uncertainty and slowed growth.

Cultural change is never easy and it is unlikely that specific policy actions can be designed for the necessary broad economic and social change. Well-functioning governments with consistent policy actions are more likely to support growth and transformation than frequent unexpected changes in policy direction. As we have argued, confidence among SME leaders matters as the technology evolves. Investment in workers talent and engagement will require considerable capital reallocation from alternative uses and, thus, increased confidence among both workers and business leaders.

- **Promote improved confidence and a positive outlook among small and medium enterprises (SMEs)**

  If income and productivity growth is to improve, economic activity must be reallocated to the most efficient firms and productivity-lagging firms must be willing to invest in the necessary skill, technology, and change management. While large enterprises have opportunities for improvement, most often SMEs lack the confidence in the long-run outlook to justify the technology adoption and investment spending necessary for future growth.

  Researchers at the Organization for Economic Cooperation and Development (OECD) find SMEs—firms with fewer than 250 employees and revenue of less than €50 million—account for over 99 percent of all firms in each country. They are diverse and vary markedly in their competitive ability, propensity to innovate, and growth potential. SMEs employ at least 60 percent of the labor force in most OECD nations. In the services sectors, a greater proportion of employment is found in SMEs than in the manufacturing sector.

For SMEs, size often acts as a barrier to adoption and, as such, smaller businesses continue to lag in digital transformation, lacking resources, awareness, necessary skills, and financing. As we have seen, successful digital transformation and migration to a cloud computing environment sets the stage of the development and deployment of AI applications. However, as we have also seen AI adoption generally remains low, especially among SMEs. Further AI technology innovation is required to reduce cost, increase ease of use, expand the pace of adoption, and open the opportunity for broad SME adoption.

To address such gaps, SMEs can source external AI expertise and solutions. Software as a Services (SaaS) and Machine Learning as a Service (MLaaS) offer advantages such as scalability, cost, technical knowledge, and embedded digital security. However, understanding AI benefits and building an effective transformation is required. Reskilling SME business leaders and workers to ensure work processes redesign and AI models training is critical (OECD 2021).

The OECD research found that certain features of national tax systems may inadvertently disadvantage SMEs relative to larger enterprises, including the asymmetric treatment of profits and losses and a bias toward debt over equity (OECD 2015). One of the most important issues affecting SMEs is the disproportionately high impact of regulatory and tax compliance, created by the significant fixed compliance costs. In some nations, SMEs have also had limited access to finance for growth and expansion since the 2008–2009 financial crisis.

In the United States, for example, the confidence of SME business leaders is remarkably sensitive to presidential administrations, presumably reflecting concern over tax and regulatory policy. Cultural and political change—among political leaders as well as business leaders—is needed to achieve tax and regulatory policy consistency, independent of political leadership. Broad social recognition of the important role SMEs play, increased policy consistency, and continued AI technology advancement will all support productivity gains among current lagging firms.

- **Encourage advances in AI technology while addressing risks and fairness issues**

    As we have shown, AI solutions have been adopted by only approximately 10 percent of potential applications. AI technology remains in its infancy. As Zolas et al. have written:

    > Despite increasingly widespread discussion in the press of machine learning, robotics, automated vehicles, natural language processing, machine vision, voice recognition and other advanced technologies, we find that their adoption rates are relatively low... We also find that technology adoption exhibits a hierarchical pattern, with the most-sophisticated technologies being present most often only when more-basic applications are as well. For instance, digitization of business information is very widely adopted. Adoption of cloud services displays an intermediate level of adoption, with a large share of firms electing to host at least one or more IT functions in the cloud. Intensive use of the cloud is slightly lower but still quite prevalent. Cloud users overwhelmingly also display a higher level of digitization. Likewise, firms reporting adoption of advanced business [AI] technologies also have predominantly adopted both digitization and cloud services, suggesting interdependencies between technology applications and potentially a cumulative progression of adoption. (See Zolas et al., 2–3)

    With much concern over job losses associated with the deployment of AI, the technology remains in much too limited deployment to account for job losses that have already occurred. Much or most of the already realized losses must be associated with the more basic digitization of business information and often from the introduction of manufacturing sector robotics. We can't blame AI technology for more than a small percentage of job losses.

Of course, the fear might be that if measurable job losses have occurred with only basic digitization of business information, more advanced AI technology will almost surely result in greater job losses going forward. While the future is uncertain and greater future job losses could occur, history suggests there is a meaningful chance that the future will differ from the recent past. As the technology becomes less expensive; easier to develop, use, and deploy; and AI solutions create greater demand for capital investment and accompany greater business model and business process innovation, more jobs could be created than are lost for a net gain. Depending on the competitive environment and the extent of creative destruction, innovation can result in more robust growth.

But the application of the technology is continuing to change. There is early data to suggest the pandemic has already reprioritized the nature of innovation and the use of the new general-interest technology. In a November 2020 survey of 6,700 C-level executives across 13 business functions, 28 industries, and 46 countries, the IBM Institute for Business Value (IBV) found a reprioritization of technology focus growing out of the pandemic. Successive analyses by the IBV have revealed that mobile apps, AI, and cloud computing provided the greatest performance impact across industries throughout the pandemic. But while capabilities around mobile apps and cloud computing are relatively mature in many organizations, those around AI typically are far from maturity. While focus on mobile apps, cloud usage, and AI solutions have increased, the shift has deprioritized Internet of things applications, along with advanced analytics and robotic process transformation (IBM Institute of Business Value 2020).

The IBV survey also found that AI offers the most significant marginal opportunity in industries such as life sciences, banking, and financial markets. The analysis revealed companies turning to AI to address pandemic-exposed vulnerabilities, such as an inability to absorb increases in customer-service volume and a need to recalibrate broken or uncertain supply chains.

As with any new technology that could reshape the future, there are risks and ethical pitfalls that could arise. The European Union has proposed a set of AI regulations that, if violated, could result in material fines, and the U.S. Federal Trade Commission (FTC) has published a notice that it could hold organizations accountable for proliferating bias or inequities through AI. The Biden Administration, as well as the current congress, has taken a more active stance in exploring potential AI regulation. Beyond regulatory risk, a number of risks have arisen—privacy, security, transparency, explainability, safety, performance, and third-party risk (Buehler, Dooley, Grennan, and Singla 2021). If AI technology is to be successful, each must be taken seriously. However, the risk that has received the most attention is fairness. Bias is easily inadvertently encoded in AI models. Data that are limited to a single group or class of consumers, or workers limits, for excluded groups, the ability of models to accurately forecast actions to be taken or recommendations to be made. While the benefit of AI technology seems likely to be realized, there is much to be done to address job losses, solution prioritization, business risks, and fairness.

- **Support deeper worker engagement between business leaders and workers**

  A large body of economic research points to productivity gains resulting from increased tangible and intangible capital investment, business model and business process innovation, and the power of creative destruction. We have made the case, based on existing research, often including random control treatment, that productivity gains respond, not only to the skill of workers but also to their engagement. Workers who feel they are treated fairly in terms of compensation and career advancement with opportunities for education and training report high levels of job satisfaction and are more productive.

  As we have argued, worker engagement is especially important in the services sectors where the skill and attitudes of workers are vital for service quality, revenue growth, worker income, and enterprise profitability. As recent research has also suggested, addressing worker's personal concerns, such as child care and transportation also appears to improve engagement. The recent wave of worker resignations, seemingly in reaction to the 2020–2021 pandemic, suggests workers are taking it upon themselves to find opportunities with improved compensation and working conditions which, if successful, could result in improved engagement and follow-on productivity gains.

Government education and training programs can help, even starting as soon as early childhood. However, much depends on the attitudes, beliefs, and values of both workers and business leaders. Many business leaders have recognized that workers in the millennial and Gen-X cohort expect greater fulfillment and satisfaction from their work experience and have adjusted work arrangements accordingly. Workers born, since 1980 in these cohorts, now make up a substantial portion of the workforce. If success is to be achieved—more robust economic and productivity growth and more equal incomes—business leaders will have to realize that a generational shift will make it in their interest to support worker engagement in new and different ways.

Finally, as we have argued, all jobs will change. We have advanced the possibility that in the deployment era of the Fourth Industrial Revolution, labor and capital will become increasingly complementary, as opposed to the substitutability of the installation era. While new technology will continue to automate tasks that many workers currently perform, the creation of new tasks and increased labor demand resulting from more robust growth and increased capital investment spending will continue to provide meaningful job opportunities for a slowly growing workforce.

- **Seek a new social contract among workers, businesses, and governments**
  Improved economic performance is only likely to be realized when workers, business leaders, and elected public officials have a view of a common interest and an ability to compromise, notwithstanding wide differences that will continue to exist. A new social contract will permit the necessary working relationships that will support growth and more vigorous income expansion.

  Shafik defines a social contract as a "partnership between individuals, businesses, civil society and the state to contribute to a system to which there are collective benefits." By contrast, the "welfare state is the mechanisms for pooling risks and investing in social benefits mediated through the political process and subsequent state actions" (Shafik 2018,10).

SMEs, because they lack the resources of large enterprises, have a broad range of unmet needs, and can realize substantial benefit from a robust ecosystem of partners. Their limited size creates a need for capabilities and resources that would make them more productive, including talented workers, technology, finance, and managerial practices. Consequently, the ecosystem of medium and large firms, business leaders, venture capital funds, and professional talent in which SMEs operate is necessary to achieve the scale required for tangible and intangible investment to generate expected returns and to achieve the market reach necessary for sustainable profitability and income flow. Early-stage innovative start-ups, established successful start-ups, growing medium-size companies, and stagnant or struggling medium-size companies are the SMEs that are most likely to benefit from ecosystem support as they acquire new talent and skill, apply new AI capabilities, and invest in the needed tangible and intangible capital.

Limited familiarity with AI, expensive talent, and constrained investment capital can slow AI adoption by SMEs. However, some governments have begun digital-productivity adoption programs to help SMEs deploy AI technologies in their processes and products. These programs often depend on an ecosystem of different players and professionals (see Albaz, Dondi, Rida, and Schubert 2020).

To facilitate the development and functioning of local ecosystems, in a novel arrangement, the UK government has established The Productivity Institute. The institute is UK-wide exploring what productivity means for businesses, workers, and communities. The institute works closely with business leaders across eight devolved regions to understand productivity issues and test practical business interventions.

The gap in productivity across UK regions is much wider than among other OECD regions. With a strong local focus, eight Regional Productivity Forums provide a platform for business leaders, academic researchers, and policy makers to work together on critical local productivity issues. The forums are involved in the design and implementation of practical business and policy interventions. Forum members include policy, community, and business leaders from local, national, and multinational enterprises. Each Productivity Forum is chaired by a regional business leader and supported by a Forum Lead from each of the partner universities.

The disease, death, and dislocation wrought by the 2020–2021 pandemic, following as it did a decade after the 2008–2009 Great Recession and financial crisis, appears to have caused many workers to rethink their relationships to their employers, their careers, and their future. The 2021 wave of worker resignations is well known. A substantial portion of workers have either quit their prepandemic job, found new jobs, or are seriously considering such a change. Increasingly, workers are choosing independent work as their primary income source or to supplement existing income. New technology requires new and different workforce skills, and workers have a range of possibilities to prepare themselves, improve their skills, or learn new ones. Likewise, the Great Recession, financial crisis, and the pandemic have caused business leaders, even those lagging in technology adoption, to begin the shift to new technology, increase innovation, realize the power of creative destruction, redesign, and restructure how work is done, and increase the pace of tangible and intangible capital investment. While transformation remains in the early stages, the missing link is the political leadership across the developed world. One can only hope that political leaders soon feel the immense pressure from workers and businesses to, similarly, change how nations are led. A new social contract is very necessary.

Epilogue | Know Unknows

In a brief book, there are inevitably important topics that cannot be covered. In this book, there are three such topics that stand out—China, demographics, and energy technology. The book does not focus on the dramatically changed role of China in the global economy over the past forty years. Rather, China's role in the global economy is important and will be more important in the years ahead.

Related to China's role in the global economy is the 2022 Russia–Ukraine war. While it's too early to fully understand the complete set of economic, diplomatic, and strategic implications, early returns suggest global supply chains will be impacted, perhaps on a long-term basis. Businesses in Europe, United Kingdom, and North America will be reconsidering alternative sources of skill, business partnerships, and manufacturing locations. Such considerations are expensive and have long-term implications. Undoubtedly, any transformation will mean the deployment of new tangible capital and new advanced digital technology.

In addition, while demographics are clearly very important and variable over long time horizons, it is beyond the scope of the current book to consider the impact in detail (see Goodhart and Pradhan 2020). Similarly, energy technology has played a vital role in each era, migrating from water to steam to electricity to fossil fuels to nonrenewables. Here is a summary of each topic.

China as the Next Global Hegemon

The opportunity in the period ahead is not lost on China's political leaders. Despite notions in the west that only democracy can promote innovation and creativity, China is challenging such thinking. As a strategic competitor, China is formidable. Weinstein (2022) makes the case that the Chinese government is attempting to create a system that promotes linkage between state-owned enterprises (SOEs) and private enterprises. Understanding the limitations facing the SOEs, China's leadership has focused on private sector innovation with government funding and research incentives enhancing innovation potential. With Chinese universities, private sector firms are having success, discrediting the notion that only democratic nations can successfully innovate. Nonetheless, China's political leaders appear to have recognized the need to combine the innovative aspects of capitalism with more rigid, traditional socialist features.

WeChat might be the best example of Chinese technological innovation. Weinstein (2022) writes, "Individuals are able to do almost anything using the app, from ordering food and paying bills to filing for divorce and applying for visas. The proliferation of WeChat throughout Chinese society—spanning generations and across the urban-rural divide—is a monumental feat and demonstrates WeChat's adaptability." WeChat's success has spawned the creation of many of the world's leading fintech companies, including Ant Financial and JD Finance.

The Chinese effort to build smarter cities is another illustration of the ability to derive innovative capabilities from preexisting technologies. After the 2008 launch of its Smarter Planet initiative, IBM helped to advance the Smarter Planet concept in China. Huawei, the Chinese Academy of Sciences, and the State Grid Corporation have all successfully deployed a wide range of Smarter Planet solutions. The Smarter Planet investments have created a domestic market opportunity of more than a trillion dollars with the three Chinese entities dominating Smarter Planet patents. However, as Weinstein observes, Smarter Planet applications in China have gone much further than those deployed elsewhere by incorporating surveillance and monitoring technologies into the broader ecosystem.

Despite fintech and Smarter Planet success, China continues to struggle to innovate in areas such as semiconductor technology and the needed complex and expensive chip manufacturing equipment. In addition, China also relies on imports for many strategically important technologies that it's unable to produce domestically, including gas turbines, high-pressure piston pumps, steel for high-end bearings, photolithography machines, and core industrial software.

China has demonstrated a capacity to innovate and compete on a global scale, but its capacity has not yet proliferated across all sectors. Limitations notwithstanding, China has developed a system through which private sector firms, universities, and government institutes learn from foreign counterparts and adapt to fill innovation gaps. It's very possible that in the decades ahead, Chinese political leaders will succeed in drawing on free market principles without surrendering control of the private sector while deploying the innovation necessary for continued rapid growth.[1]

Demographic Slowdown Constrains Growth

Economic growth is the product of labor force growth and productivity growth. With labor force growth limited by developed nation population growth, productivity growth takes on increased importance, with some automation necessary to meet growing labor demand.

In the United States, for example, the most recent population estimates from the U.S. Census Bureau indicate that population growth from 2010 to 2020 was the second lowest in the nation's history, 0.7 percent per year. Among all 50 states, 37 grew more slowly in the 2010s than in the previous decade, and three states lost population. The largest number of such states since the 1980s. The decade brought declines in the number of births, increases in the number of deaths, and lower immigration rates. Immigration was reduced due to federal restrictions that led to a decline in the noncitizen foreign-born population. In the 12 months, from mid-2020 to mid-2021, the U.S. population grew at an unprecedented low of just 0.1 percent.

The most recent census also found for the first time, there was a decade-long loss in the number of white Americans who do not identify with other racial and ethnic groups. All the U.S. population growth over the decade is attributable to people of color. Those identifying as Latino or Hispanic, Black, Asian American, Native Hawaiian or Pacific Islander, Native American, and as two or more races now comprise more than 40 percent of the U.S. population. The nation's under-18 cohort experienced an absolute decline of more than one million. The decline was the

---

[1] Lee (2018) imagines China and the United States forming a new AI duopoly with workers finding new ways of working along with Chinese and American political leaders struggling with the changing economic landscape.

result of a loss in the white youth population that was not fully offset by gains in other racial and ethnic groups. As a result, white Americans now comprise less than half of the nation's under-age-18 population.

The United States is not alone in experiencing slow population and labor force growth. Very low birth rates in Europe and parts of eastern Asia, and the resultant population decrease, have received considerable attention. In the 2010 decade, the European Union's population growth was 0.1 percent per year. Labor force shortages are widely recognized, particularly among service occupations.

Asia and Europe are home to some of the world's oldest populations, those aged 65 and above. At 28 percent, Japan has the oldest population followed by Italy at 23 percent. Finland, Portugal, and Greece complete the top five at just under 22 percent. Southern Europe, which includes such countries as Croatia, Greece, Italy, Malta, Portugal, Serbia, Slovenia, and Spain, is the oldest region in the world with 21 percent of the population aged 65 and above.

However, the world's most populist nations are not among the oldest. Twelve percent of China's population is aged 65 or above, 16 percent of the United States is in the older age group, and 6 percent in India is in the older cohort (www.prb.org/resources/global-aging-and-the-demographic-divide/).

Global Warming and the Transformation to Renewable Energy

Finally, each industrial revolution has brought with it a new energy technology. From waterpower, to steam, to electricity, to fossil fuels, each has played a primary role in successive revolutions. However, the consequences of these earlier technologies, most importantly fossil fuels, have been massive climate change and global warming. It's very likely that renewable energy sources will play an important role in the period ahead with fossil fuels diminishing in importance and renewable sources, over the long term, reducing energy costs. However, the transformation will not be easy or quick.

Recent work by Fries (2021) outlines the challenges, actions, and policies that will be necessary. Fries' perspective on the renewable energy transformation ahead is through the lens of the policy and the investment decisions to be taken by governments, businesses, and households. But changing the current fossil-fuel-based system to low-carbon alternatives is among the most difficult challenges the global community currently faces.

McKinsey Global Institute (2022) estimates that tangible capital spending on physical assets for energy and land-use systems in the net-zero transition between 2021 and 2050 will be approximately $275 trillion, or $9.2 trillion per year, an annual increase of $3.5 trillion per year from current spending levels.

Fries writes: "Much as an 'industrial enlightenment' of scientific knowledge and its engineering application enlivened the first and second industrial revolutions and created modern energy systems, the awakening of low-carbon technologies today emerges from investments in knowledge and new capabilities". In the advanced industrialized nations, including China and Russia, the shift to renewable energy requires almost every business and household to invest in low-carbon alternatives with suppliers transforming energy production.

While there is broad agreement in economics on (1) using emissions pricing to internalize environmental externalities and (2) government policy support for research and development (R&D), in practice, achieving the levels and scope of adequate emissions pricing has been challenging. Incomplete markets, adverse distributional impacts, arbitrary political shifts, and time inconsistencies in policy implementation have all contributed to unsuccessful policy transformation.

In Fries view, markets are unlikely to deliver the needed change for three reasons.

- Knowledge spillovers arise not only from R&D activities but also from deploying and using low-carbon technologies— learning from experience.
- Some low-carbon technologies benefit from substantial scale economies, especially those that can be mass produced with potential for wide deployment across sectors and countries.
- At the core of the transformation are government-designed and government-regulated markets for electric power.

Fries recommends a focus on not only emissions pricing but also nonprice policy interventions such as market-creating and industry-supporting policies for low-carbon technologies, especially during their early deployment in initial markets. Adapting government-designed energy markets, their regulations and infrastructures to low-carbon alternatives is essential.

Appendix A

Dating Major Global Financial Crises

Both of the most recent major global financial crises—1930s and 2000s—followed close behind the peaks in the Kelly et al. innovation index. Perez cites the mass production process that permitted the building of the Ford Motor Company's Model-T in 1908 as the signature innovation of the early 20th century, ultimately providing rapid growth of the 1920s and the mania that ensued (see Gordon 2016, 149–168). Later in the century, it was Intel's microprocessor that made computing and communications at scale possible, and that gave rise to the current era.

While both of these technological innovations have gone on to demonstrate long-run success, in the excitement following their creation, the frenzy, and mania—the roaring 20s and the dot.com bubble—eventually resulted in a separation of current period pricing and long-run fundamentals. The ensuing asset price correction and write down of debt, which financed such asset purchases, resulted in painful balance sheet adjustments that required deep recessions to correct.

While the 1929–1933 global depression and the 2008–2010 global financial crisis are well known, the 19th-century's major financial crises are less well known. Further, available data describing the period are relatively sparce and are very limited for the early decades of the century.[1]

The 1890 peak in the Kelly et al. innovation index is followed by a financial crisis aligning with the 1893–1894 recession as dated in the National Bureau of Economic Research (NBER) chronology (see Table A.1). Both Perez and Aliber–Kindleberger designate the recession as

---

[1] The Kelly et al. innovation index is limited by the lack of available patent data prior to 1840. Portions of the Reinhart–Rogoff financial crisis data extend back to 1800. Aliber, Kindleberger, and Perez are economic historians and provide qualitative descriptions for earlier centuries.

Table A.1 Major financial crisis dates

Peak	Trough	Contraction Peak to trough	Expansion Previous trough to this peak	Cycle Trough from previous trough	Cycle Peak from previous peak	Kelly et. al innovation peak	Perez	Aliber-Kindleberger	Reinhart-Rogoff
Quarterly dates are in parentheses									
Pre-NBER chronology	1793–1794						Crisis	Crisis	
	1825–1826							Crisis	Crisis
	1848–1850						Crisis	Crisis	
	December 1854 (IV)	-	-	-	-				
June 1857 (II)	December 1858 (IV)	18	30	48	-				
October 1860 (III)	June 1861 (III)	8	22	30	40				
April 1865 (I)	December 1867 (I)	32	46	78	54				
June 1869 (II)	December 1870 (IV)	18	18	36	50	Peak			
October 1873 (III)	March 1879 (I)	65	34	99	52				
March 1882 (I)	May 1885 (II)	38	36	74	101				
March 1887 (II)	April 1888 (I)	13	22	35	60				
July 1890 (III)	May 1891 (II)	10	27	37	40	Peak			
January 1893 (I)	June 1894 (II)	17	20	37	30		Crisis	Crisis	
December 1895 (IV)	June 1897 (II)	18	18	36	35				
June 1899 (III)	December 1900 (IV)	18	24	42	42				
September 1902 (IV)	August 1904 (III)	23	21	44	39				
May 1907 (II)	June 1908 (II)	13	33	46	56			Crisis	Crisis
January 1910 (I)	January 1912 (IV)	24	19	43	32				
January 1913 (I)	December 1914 (IV)	23	12	35	36				
August 1918 (III)	March 1919 (I)	7	44	51	67				
January 1920 (I)	July 1921 (III)	18	10	28	17				
May 1923 (II)	July 1924 (III)	14	22	36	40				
October 1926 (III)	November 1927 (IV)	13	27	40	41				
August 1929 (III)	March 1933 (I)	43	21	64	34	Peak	Crisis	Crisis	Crisis
May 1937 (II)	June 1938 (II)	13	50	63	93				
February 1945 (I)	October 1945 (IV)	8	80	88	93				
November 1948 (IV)	October 1949 (IV)	11	37	48	45				
July 1953 (II)	May 1954 (II)	10	45	55	56				
August 1957 (III)	April 1958 (II)	8	39	47	49				
April 1960 (II)	February 1961 (I)	10	24	34	32				
December 1969 (IV)	November 1970 (IV)	11	106	117	116				
November 1973 (IV)	March 1975 (I)	16	36	52	47				
January 1980 (I)	July 1980 (III)	6	58	64	74				
July 1981 (III)	November 1982 (II)	16	12	28	18				
July 1990 (III)	March 1991 (I)	8	92	100	108				
March 2001 (I)	November 2001 (IV)	8	120	128	128	Peak			
December 2007 (IV)	June 2009 (II)	18	73	91	81		Crisis	Crisis	Crisis

a major global financial crisis. Aliber–Kindleberger and Reinhart–Rogoff designate the 1907–1908 recession as a follow-on major global financial crisis as balance sheets were cleansed for the explosive growth ahead.

Perez points to the 1875 opening of the Carnegie Bessemer Pittsburgh steel plant as the instantiation of the innovation that drove the surge. Perez describes the era at the turn of the century as one in which distributed electrical power for industrial production was introduced.[2] Perez writes that economies of scale were created with massive steel structures for vertically integrated plants. Universal standardization and cost accounting were introduced for control and efficiency. Science became a productive force.

---

[2] David (1990) and earlier papers describe the process of industrial electrification in detail. See also Gordon 2016, pp. 114–122. After the very significant technology deployment of the 1870s, Gordon (2016, p. 61) concludes: "The Second Industrial Revolution was on its way to changing the world beyond recognition."

While data for the early decades of the 19th century are very limited, there is consensus that the building of the rail networks across continental Europe, Britain, and the United States resulted as a mania at mid-century. Aliber–Kindleberger and Perez detail the 1848–1850 panic that followed the railroad mania. Aliber–Kindleberger (2015, 192) write: "In January 1847 distress developed in London in response to railroad calls and the crisis came late in the summer."

Perez suggests that the 1829 test of the "rocket" steam engine for the Liverpool–Manchester railway began a series of innovations that resulted in economies of agglomeration and the creation of industrial cities, scale from standard parts and machine-made machines, and steam as an energy source. Crafts (2004) finds "steam contributed little to growth before 1830 .... Only with the advent of high-pressure steam after 1850 did the technology realise its potential."

Mokyr cites important innovations in the late 18th and early 19th centuries resulting from unskilled-bias technology: "First in firearms, then in clocks, pumps, locks, mechanical reapers, typewriters, sewing machines, and eventually in engines and bicycles, interchangeable parts technology proved superior and replaced the skilled artisans working with chisel and file" (see Mokyr 1990, 137, cited in Acemoglu 2020).

Appendix B

Long-Lived Capital With Embedded Tangible and Intangible Capital

The embodiment of innovation, ideas, and technology in capital investment—both tangible and intangible—has been among the most notable features of the four industrial revolutions. The nature of technological embodiment has been a source of periodic controversy in the economics literature. Putty-clay capital was studied in the 1960s, and received renewed attention in the 1990s and 2000s (see Hercowitz 1998, Cullenberg and Dasgupta 2001 and Gilchrist and Williams 2002).

With putty-clay capital, the ex ante production technology allows substitution between capital and labor. Ex post, however, productivity is determined by the embodied vintage technology and the fixed choice of capital intensity. In a putty-clay model, capital is replaced with capital that has greater capacity than the depreciated capital.[1] The purchase of new capital only affects the productivity of the workers using the new capital. It leaves the productivity of workers using legacy capital unaffected. The new capital does not impact the productivity of existing capital.[2]

---

[1] Originally introduced by Johansen (1959), putty-clay technology breaks the tight restriction on short-run production possibilities imposed by Cobb–Douglas technology and provides a natural framework for examining issues related to irreversible investment. However, an impediment to the adoption of the putty-clay framework has been the analytic difficulty associated with a model in which all existing vintages of capital are tracked.

[2] In the neoclassical production function, output is a function of labor hours, and the capital stock. Any investment affects the marginal productivity of all labor and existing capital. Empirical investment behavior supports the assumption of ex post fixed proportions (clay) over the assumption of ex post variable proportions (putty). See Lasky (2003).

To understand the influences of growth, productivity, technology, and depreciation on investment spending, Lasky (2003) builds a model of investment spending in which the desired change in output capacity is a function of net additions to capacity, the growth in capacity from existing capital, and the difference in output from replacement capital and the capital replaced. The implication, by simple arithmetic, is that net additions to capacity—represented by an investment equation—equals the desired change in capacity minus both the increase in capacity from replacing depreciating capital with new capital and the gains in productive capacity from existing capital.

Let $N_{e,t}$ be the units of expansion capital of each type put in place at time t. Let $R_{m,t,i}$ be the units of capital of type m and age i depreciating at time t. Let y_t be the average output during period t of workers using only capital existing before time t. Let $y^h_{m,t,i}$ be the hypothetical output of a worker using a unit of capital of type m aged i years at time t had it not depreciated at time t.[3]

Let $y_{m,t+i,i}$ denote the output at time $t+i$ of a worker using capital of type m aged i periods at time $t+i$.

$$y_{m,t+i,i} = A_{t+i}U_{t+i}G_{m,t+i}\left(k_{m,t}\right)^{\alpha} \tag{B.1}$$

where A_{t+i} is economywide technology, U_{t+i} is the effect of economywide intensity of usage, or effort, on productivity, $G_t(\ )$ is the function aggregating different types of capital, k_{m+t} is the size of capital of type m in constant dollars used by worker n at time t, and a is capital's coefficient in the production function. There are M types of capital.

---

[3] Lasky (2013) presents $N_{e,t}$ and $R_{m,t,i}$ as the number of machines for expansion and replacement. Also, $k_{m,t}$ is the size of machine type m used by worker n at time t. The assumption is that every worker uses a similar, although not identical, mix of different types of plant and equipment. Lasky's exclusion of intangible capital limits the model for current purposes. Here the assumption is that there is both tangible and intangible capital. $N_{e,t}$ and $R_{m,t,i}$ are units of capital for expansion and replacement and $k_{m,i}$ is the size of capital of type m in constant dollars used by worker n at time t.

Let y_t be period t output of workers using only capital existing before time t. If new capital was the same size as existing capital, expansion capacity would be $N_{e,t}y_t$. However, if new capital differs in size from existing capital, output will differ from that of existing capital. The output of expansion capital can be expressed as

$$N_{e,t}y_t\left[1+\sum_{m=1}^{M}\left(\frac{y_{m,t,0}}{y_t}-1\right)\right] \tag{B.2}$$

In a putty-clay world, the output of replacement capital is generally larger than the output of a worker using depreciated capital. Let $R_{m,t,i}$ be units of capital of type m and age i depreciating at time t and let L_m be the service life of capital of type m. The total replacement capital of type m:

$$R_{m,t}=\int_0^{L_m}R_{m,t,i}di \tag{B.3}$$

At time t, the increase in capacity obtained by replacing depreciated capital of all types with new capital is:

$$\sum_{m=1}^{M}R_{m,t}y_{m,t,0}-\sum_{m=1}^{M}\int_{i=0}^{L_m}R_{m,t,i}y_{m,t,i}^b di \tag{B.4}$$

Let $\dot{A}_t$ be annualized growth of technology at time t. Then the rate of increase of capacity due to technology growth at time t is:

$$\left(\dot{A}_t\Big/A_t\right)N_ty_t \tag{B.5}$$

where N_t is the total capital of each type at time t. Let $\dot{YE}_t$ be the desired change in output at time t. Output per worker from new investment is:

$$N_{e,t}y_t\left[1+\sum_{m=1}^{M}\left(\frac{y_{m,t,0}}{y_t}-1\right)\right]$$
$$=\dot{YE}_t-\sum_{m=1}^{M}R_{m,t}y_{m,t,0}+\sum_{m=1}^{M}\int_{i=0}^{L_m}R_{m,t,i}y_{m,t,i}^b di-\left(\dot{A}_t\Big/A_t\right)N_ty_t \tag{B.6}$$

Adding $R_{m,t} y_{m,t,0}$, output of type m replacement capital, to both sides of equation (B.6), yields the output of new capital of type M:

$$\left(N_{e,t} + R_{M,t}\right) y_{M,t,0}$$

$$= \dot{Y}E_t + R_{M,t} y_t - \left(\dot{A_t}\Big/A_t\right) N_t y_t$$

$$-N_{e,t} \sum_{m=1}^{M} \left(y_{m,t,0} - y_t\right) + R_{M,t}\left(y_{m,t,0} - y_t\right) \qquad (B.7)$$

$$-\sum_{m=1}^{M} R_{m,t} y_{m,t,0} + \sum_{m=1}^{M} \int_{i=0}^{L_m} R_{m,t,i} y_{m,t,i}^b \, di$$

The first line of equation (B.7) to the right of the equal sign indicates the capacity of workers using new capital as the desired change in capacity plus the capacity of depreciated capital less the change in capacity from using improved technology with existing capital. The second line adjusts for the net output of new machines. The third line adjusts for the net output of existing machines.

To specify the investment equation, output per worker $y_{M,t,o}$ in equation (B.7) is replaced with the size of new capital of type M. Businesses choose the units of capital that maximize expected profits. The optimal units of capital depend on output per worker and the cost of capital.

The present discounted value of profits associated with a new unit of capital of type m purchased and put into service at time t is:

$$\pi^*_{m,t} = \int_0^{L_m} \left(p_{t+i} y_{m,t+i,i}, F_{t,i}\right) di - q_{m,t} k_{m,t} \qquad (B.8)$$

where p_t is the price of output y_t, F is the discount factor:

$$F_{t,i} = e^{-\int_0^i r_{t+j} \, dj}$$

For the nominal rate of return r_{t+j} at time t, $q_{m,t}$ is the purchase price of new capital of type m. Setting the derivative of the expected profit function (B.8) to zero and solving for $q_{m,t}$ yields:

$$q_{m,t} = \int_0^{L_m} \left(\check{p}_{t+i} \frac{\delta \check{y}_{m,t+i,i}}{\delta k_{m,t}} \check{F}_{t,i}\right) di \qquad (B.9)$$

where a circumflex over a variable indicates an expected value.

If $\dfrac{\delta y}{\delta k}$ is replaced with the elasticity of the capital aggregator, G, with respect to the change in the size of the i-year-old type m capital at time $t+i$

$$s_{m,t+i,i} = \frac{\delta ln G_{m,t+i}(k_{m,t})}{\delta ln k_{m,t}}$$

then, the first-order condition is:

$$q_{m,t} = \int_0^{L_m} \left(\check{p}_{t+i} \alpha_t s_{m,t+i,i} \frac{\check{y}_{m,t+i,i}}{k_{m,t}} \check{F}_{t,i} \right) di \qquad (B.10)$$

where $\alpha_t s_{m,t+i,l}$ is the share of the present discounted value of the expected output to be produced by the work using the new capital that equates with the cost of new capital. If $s_{m,t+i,l}$ is constant over time:

$$q_{m,t} k_{m,t} = \alpha s_{m,t,0} p_t y_{m,t,o} \int_0^{L_m} e^{(\dot{p}_t + \dot{y}_m - r)} di \qquad (B.11)$$

Evaluating the integral and solving for $k_{m,t}$ yields the optimal size of capital units:

$$k_{m,t} = \alpha s_{m,t,0} \frac{p_t}{v_{m,t}} y_{m,t,o} \qquad (B.12)$$

where $v_{m,t}$ is the cost of capital:

$$v_{m,t} = q_{m,t} \frac{r - \dot{p}_t - \dot{y}_m}{1 - e^{[-(r-\dot{p}_t-\dot{y}_m)L_m]}} \qquad (B.13)$$

For simplification, rewriting equation (B.7):

$$\left(N_{e,t} + R_{M,t} \right) y_t = \dot{Y} E_t + R_{M,t} y_t - \left(\dot{A}\Big/A_t \right) N_t y_t + NONC + NOEC$$

$$(B.14)$$

where $NONC$ is net output of new capital and $NOEC$ is net output of existing capital. Investment in capital of type m at time t:

$$I_{m,t} = \left(N_{e,t} + R_{M,t} \right) k_{m,t} \qquad (B.15)$$

Substituting for $k_{m,t}$ from equation (B.12), dividing by y_t, and substituting for $(N_{e,t} + R_{M,t})$ yields:

$$I_{m,t} = \alpha s_{m,t,0} \frac{p_t}{v_{m,t}} \frac{y_{m,t,0}}{y_t} \left[\dot{Y}E_t + R_{M,t}y_t - \left(\frac{\dot{A}_t}{A_t} \right) N_t y_t + NONC + NOEC \right]$$

(B.16)

Investment in capital of type m is a function of (1) the elasticity of output with respect to capital of type m, (2) the ratio of the output price to the cost of capital, (3) the increment of desired capacity growth from capital type m, (4) desired capacity growth, (5) replacement demand, (6) growth in technology, and (7) the net gain from net new and existing capital.

With (B.16), the impact of demand and productivity shocks on investment spending can be considered. Somewhat surprisingly, the model is explicit about the impact of technology on investment but treats the impact of changes in TFP indirectly. Technology, A, alters the output delivered per unit of capital. Similarly, improved technology can also reduce $q_{m,t}$, the purchase price of capital. TFP, as is the standard definition, alters output as resources are collectively utilized in alternative configurations. Changes in technology and TFP do not, in principle, need to be associated or causally related.[4]

---

[4] If TFP captures, for example, improved management practices or business model innovation, improved capital technology—for example, increased computing power or advances in software technology—may or may not result in output and investment increases depending on how resources are combined. The distinction between the success of management practices and information technology investment has been the focus of Bloom, Van Reenen and collaborators across a substantial body of work. See Bloom, Sadun, and Van Reenen (2012). Bloom and Van Reenen (2007) find measures of managerial practice are strongly associated with firm-level productivity, profitability, Tobin's Q, sales growth, and survival rates. They calculate that product market competition and family firms account for about half of the gap in management practices between the United States and France and one-third of the gap between the United States and the United Kingdom.

In (B.16), an increase in TFP could cause a proportionate rise in output and thus in investment. TFP could also affect the cost of capital relative to the output price. For example, if higher productivity leads to lower inflation and interest rates, real interest rates and the real cost of capital could decline. Similarly, improved TFP could increase the output of existing capital, reducing the need for investment. Conversely, if output falls sufficiently or the cost of capital increases, or both, a TFP decrease could reduce investment, possibility even in the face improving technology.

A demand shock is defined as a change in $\dot{Y}E$ independent of other terms in (B.16) with an increase in demand resulting in an increase in capacity. Of course, in a dynamic context, the persistence of the demand-induced investment increase will depend on the response of prices, interest rates, and the cost of capital.

Applying the investment equation to the industrial revolution periods, the installation period, most recently 1975 to 2010, is characterized by (1) aging capital following substantial capital investment spending in the preceding deployment period, (2) a new technology, nascent at the outset of the period reaching maturity later in the period, and (3) focused business model innovation. Such conditions could suggest slower investment spending growth. One consequence is increased obsolescence of tangible and intangible capital as technology advances, driving heterogeneity in cross-sectional profitability and firm-level productivity. At the aggregate level, capital is reallocated with restructuring costs affecting the overall benefit of innovation.

Conversely, the deployment period, for example 1945 to 1975, is characterized by (1) a mature, low-cost technology and (2) rapid business model innovation. The combination of a demand shock and a productivity shock would result in substantial capital investment and, eventually, resulting in a younger capital stock.

Other evidence of the periodic de-linkage of technological innovation and increased TFP growth can be found in the economics literature. The influence of innovation on TFP—capturing, for example improved management practices, business model innovation and new product and service offerings—manifest over long periods. Over a 5- to 10-year horizon, the Kelly et al. innovation index is a strong predictor of TFP, for which a one-standard deviation increase in the index is associated with a 0.5 to 2 percentage point higher annual productivity growth.

In addition, Liu, Fernald and Basu, 2012 find that output, consumption, investment, and labor hours rise in response to improvements in consumer-goods technology but all decline following similar improvement in investment-goods technology. Basu, Fernald, and Liu show that the effects are consistent with the predictions of a two-sector dynamic stochastic general equilibrium (DSGE) model with sticky prices in each sector. The assumption that investment goods prices are costly to adjust helps fit the evidence that the relative price of investment goods adjusts slowly to shocks.

Appendix C

Capital Investment and Income Generation

Capital is not only long lived but also income generating. By its nature, capital investment is intended to generate income. As the capital stock expands, and the service it renders grows, income generation grows as well. The resulting income, of course, is earned by the owners of capital, not labor. The long-lived nature of capital and its income-generating ability can result in prolonged period of capital income production. Consequently, a substantial shift in the distribution of income between labor and capital is observed in the deployment period.

As the stock of capital expanded over the 1944–1974 deployment period, the complementary of labor and capital increased labor's income as massive industrial and business transformation, not only deployed a vast quantity of tangible and intangible capital but also drove a substantial increase in the demand for labor. The result was an increase in labor's income share. See Figure 4.1—U.S. nonresidential net fixed investment and U.S. top 1 percent income share.

However, as the deployment period of the Third Industrial Revolution became the installation period of the Fourth Industrial Revolution, the long-lived capital of the prior era continued to provide services and generate income. Capital services are derived from the stock of tangible and intangible assets. Such services differ from the capital stock because short-lived assets, such as equipment, provide more service per unit than long-lived assets, such as structures. Unlike the stock of tangible and intangible assets, capital services are owned by those providing the service.[1]

---

[1] See Bureau of Labor Statistics Glossary.

Capital services are:

$$cs_t = \left(\frac{1}{age_t}\right) + \frac{I_t - \delta_t}{K_t} \qquad (C.1)$$

where

cs_t = Capital Services
age_t = Age of Capital
I_t = Investment in new capital
δ_t = depreciation of capital
K_t = Capital Stock

Longer-lived and older assets deliver less service, while shorter-lived and younger assets deliver more service. In addition, the current period net additions are the most productive service delivery providers. Figure 2.3 shows the net additions to the capital stock and Figures 2.6, 2.7, and 2.8 show the age of the capital stock.

To measure the impact that capital services have on wealth as well as their influence on income distribution, household financial assets are estimated as a function of capital services, equity market values, and real interest rates.

$$\frac{fha_t}{sfa_t} = F\left(cs_t, s \& p_t, r_t\right) \qquad (C.2)$$

where

fha_t = Annual Net Additions of Household Financial Assets
sha_t = Current Period Stock of Financial Assets
$s\&p_t$ = Rate of Change of S&P 500 Index
r_t = Real U.S. Long-term Treasury Rate

Figure C.1 shows the ratio of net new household assets to the stock of assets. Figure C.2 shows both capital services along with the household assets ratio. Figure C.3 financial market return metrics. All data enter equation (C.2) and are represented as Hodrick–Prescott (HP) trends.

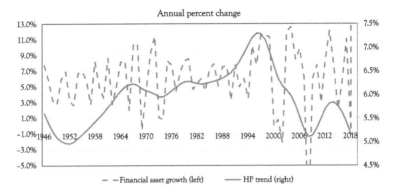

Figure C.1 U.S. household and nonprofit asset growth as a percent of fixed assets

Source: Households and nonprofit organizations; Total financial assets, Financial Accounts of the United States, Z.1, Federal Reserve Board.

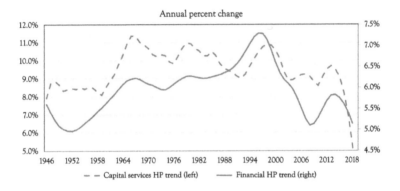

Figure C.2 U.S. household and nonprofit asset growth as a percent of fixed assets and capital services

Sources: Financial Assets, see Figure C.1, Capital services, Figures 3 (Nonresidential net capital investment), 6 (Age total and 3 categories), and 7 (Age adjusted).

Table C.1 provides estimates of equation (C.2) over four time periods. In three of the four periods, capital services are highly correlated with household assets, suggesting that the income-generating capability of tangible and intangible assets is important for the accumulation of household financial assets. Over the entire period, 1946 to 2018, and the most recent period, 1987 to 2018, the coefficient estimates are stable and

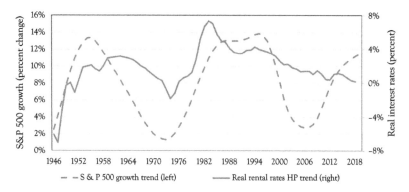

Figure C.3 U.S. real long-term treasury rates and S&P 500 growth

Sources: S&P 500, Federal Reserve Bank of St. Louis, FRED Economic Data; U.S. real long-term interest rates, 1946–1964, NBER Series 13033 from U.S. Treasury Department, Treasury Bulletin; 1965–2018, Federal Reserve Bank of St. Louis, FRED Economic Data, 10-Year treasury constant maturity rate, percent, monthly, not seasonally adjusted.

with the expected signs. In the 1987–2018 period, equity market value changes are highly correlated with household financial asset values and, at the margin, add to explainability of household financial asset accumulation. Similarly, real interest rates have also added to household wealth.

In the 1946–1974 period—the years most closely aligned with the Third Industrial Revolution deployment period—capital services are highly correlated with changes in household financial assets. During the near 30 years of capital deepening, the income generation very likely provided a source of household financial assets. The 1946–1975 period was one of strong growth in the real sector while the equity market apparently was anticipating slower growth in the period ahead, which, to some extent, turned out to be correct. The coefficient on the S&P 500 term has a negative sign and is significantly different from zero. Real interest rates rose over the period as increasing demand for financial capital contributed to the increase in financial assets while also, presumably, as contributed to the eventual slowdown in growth and capital deepening.

Secondly, the 1975–2007 period, the income generated from capital services are only weakly correlated with household asset values while changing equity market values are more highly correlated. The 1975–2007 period—the installation period of the Fourth Industrial

Table C.1 *Household financial asset flows as a percent of household asset stock*

	Household financial asset flows as a percent of household asset stock											
	1946-2018			1946-1974			1975-2007			1987-2018		
Intercept	0.0250	0.0159	0.0189	0.0234	0.0320	0.0542	0.0379	0.0394	0.0359	0.0216	0.0176	0.0280
t-statistic	5.3824	3.5038	3.3237	6.6984	5.9069	8.0464	3.3249	4.8146	5.2822	2.6915	3.4561	4.8665
Capital services	0.3624	0.4122	0.3837	0.3503	0.2794	0.0801	0.2611	0.1783	0.2143	0.4282	0.3756	0.2547
t-statistic	7.4709	9.3486	7.0172	9.4791	5.6091	1.3135	2.2191	2.1459	3.0958	4.9836	6.8804	3.9999
S&P 500	–	0.0536	0.0439	–	-0.0265	-0.0843	–	0.0753	0.1225	–	0.0991	0.0612
t-statistic	–	4.6239	2.7417	–	-2.0042	-4.9292	–	5.8308	7.5716	–	6.8425	3.3551
Real rates	–	–	0.0249	–	–	0.0862	–	–	-0.1371	–	–	0.1857
t-statistic	–	–	0.8834	–	–	4.2318	–	–	-3.8756	–	–	2.9344
R-square	0.4401	0.5711	0.5759	0.7689	0.7999	0.8834	0.1371	0.5955	0.7335	0.4529	0.7907	0.8400
F	55.8142	46.6082	31.2348	89.8541	51.9551	63.1302	4.9245	22.0826	26.6085	24.8360	54.7944	48.9866
Significance F	1.596E-10	1.3542E-13	7.2057E-13	4.4168E-10	8.2660E-10	8.3746E-12	3.3930E-02	1.2700E-06	1.7948E-08	2.4403E-05	1.4116E-10	2.8895E-11
Observations	73	73	73	29	29	29	33	33	33	32	32	32

Revolution—realized less benefit from the capital services in place from the earlier period. Meanwhile, equity market gains—as rents from the new technology are captured—were highly correlated with gains in household financial assets. With real interest rates in a long period of decline during the 32 years, the coefficient is negative sign and is significantly different from zero (See Saez and Zucman 2020).

The long-lived nature of capital assets means embodied vintage technology remains in place for an extended period. The long life also means the capital stock requires replacement infrequently, resulting in extended periods of adjustment. Further, the income-generating capability of capital services provides a long-lasting source of income and wealth. Prior to 1975, capital services were highly correlated with financial asset accumulation. In the post-1975 period, equity and debt assets—perhaps the fruit of the earlier period—are highly correlated with asset accumulation while income generating capital services recede in their correlation.

Appendix D

Shifting Labor Income Shares in the First Industrial Revolution

Shifting capital and labor income shares were a dynamic element in early industrial revolutions. Allen (2009) identifies "Engels' Pause" as the period that aligns with the First Industrial Revolution's installation period.[1] Allen shows the UK economy passed through a two-stages evolution—remarkably similar to the installation and deployment periods—characterized by fluctuations in profitability, real wages, productivity, and capital investment.

Allen asserts that the prime movers of the First Industrial Revolution were 18th-century UK technology innovations, including mechanical spinning, coke smelting, iron puddling, and the steam engine. After 1800, the revolutionized industries were large enough to affect the national economy. The macroeconomic impact was strengthened by rising agriculture sector productivity and inventions such as the power loom, the railroad, and the application of steam power generally (Crafts 2004). The adoption of the new technology led to increased capital investment—for cities, housing, and infrastructure as well as for plant and equipment.[2]

However, Britain's income shares during the First Industrial Revolution as estimated by Crafts (2021a) and Allen (2009) are relatively constant during the installation period, in contrast to the decline in labor income shares during the Fourth Industrial Revolution.

Acemoglu (2002) argues that technological change in the late 18th and early 19th centuries may have been biased *toward* unskilled labor.

---

[1] Crafts and Harley (1992) address measurement associates with UK economic growth in the 18th and 19th centuries.

[2] Bessen (2003) traces a similar path of U.S. 19th-century technology development.

There was (1) a large migration of unskilled workers from English villages and Ireland to English cities and (2) a large increase in population. The emergence of the most "skill-replacing" technology, the factory system, coincided with a substantial change in the relative supply of workers and increased demand for those unskilled workers in the new factory system, the product of the "invention of a new method of invention." These innovations—the factory system and new methods of inventions—constitute significant innovation much like innovations surrounding social media, e-commence, and search in the current period.

Crafts (2021a) also focuses on increased population growth and labor supply. Crafts and Mills find that fertility and mortality shocks between the 1760s and the 1820s raised the crude birth rate and lowered the crude death rate both by about 6 percentage points. In the circumstances of other periods, such increases would have led to real wage declines. In the context of the industrial revolution, the implication was that the population increase severely inhibited the scope for productivity growth to raise real wages.

The workforce increase created profit opportunities for firms introducing technologies that could be used with unskilled workers—often women and children. The advent of steam power and the expansion of freight and passenger rail travel across Britain and the continent expanded the scope and scale of available markets. To meet the unprecedented increase in demand and market opportunity, the incentive to replace skilled artisans with unskilled laborers was a major objective of technological improvements over the period.

Acemoglu's framework is consistent with the notion that the incentives for skill-replacing technologies were shaped by the large increase in the supply of unskilled workers. With such an increase, Acemoglu's model suggests short-run real wage declines were followed, as markets expanded over the long run, by wage increases. Thus, the constancy of labor's income share.

Allen (2009) also points to the significance of increased relative supply. Allen simulates the counterfactual that eliminates the population explosion that accompanied industrial revolution. Both output per worker and the real wage from 1770 to 1860 trend upward, with little lag of wages behind output after the increase in productivity growth in 1801.

"Engel's pause" in real wage growth is eliminated with simulated shares changing very little.

Crafts (2021a) also advances a counterfactual and finds that:

> In the absence of both these shocks [fertility and mortality], the model estimates that average real earnings growth would have been increased by 1 percentage point per year [more] between 1780 and 1840, by which time real earnings would have been more than double the 1780 level.

The counterfactuals suggest that demographic shocks that raised population growth to a new high during Britain's First Industrial Revolution undermined its potential to raise real wages. The constancy of British labor's income share in the early 19th century highlights the point that labor's income share is the product of the average wage rate, labor force participation, and population. Migration of workers from the agricultural sector to the industrial sector adds to the available workforce independent of population growth. Increased participation of unskilled labor can hold labor's share constant while the average wage rate is declining.

Appendix E

Technology and Changing Elasticity of Substitution

The social and economic benefits of AI depend on whether applications augment human activity or automate human activity. When AI augments activity, the solution complements the effort of humans, creating capabilities and enabling activities that were previously not possible. In complementing human activity, the skill and contribution of human labor retains value with compensation rising for those tasks well-suited for human skill. Conversely, when AI automates activity, the technology substitutes for human activity, workers lose employment opportunities and income. The result is a reduction in the share of income earned by labor and increased capital income, benefiting entrepreneurs and executives.

Brynjolfsson (2022) observes that a common fallacy is the assumption that all productivity-enhancing innovation automates human labor. As a counter illustration, Brynjolfsson cites the example of the jet engine. With its invention, pilot productivity grew immensely, as measured by passenger-miles per pilot hour. Instead of reducing the number of employed pilots, the technology resulted in an enormous increase in the demand for air travel, not creating more pilot jobs but employment for an entire industry.

In contrast, as has been well documented, industrial robots have resulted in reduced manufacturing sector employment and wages while boosting productivity (Acemoglu and Restrepo 2019, 2020). While AI remains in early and limited application, ICT applications—whether automating or augmenting human effort—results in shifts in the share of income earned by labor and capital.

Since Hicks (1932), the relationship between the labor share of income and the capital–labor ratio has been measured with the elasticity of substitution. To quantify the relationship between labor's income share and the capital–labor ratio, the elasticity of substitution (σ) measures the percentage change in the capital–labor ratio compared to the percentage change in the real wage–real interest rate ratio.

Acemoglu (2002) develops a simple framework to analyze the forces that shape the biases of technological change toward a particular factor. A market effect and a price effect are identified as major forces effecting equilibrium bias. The market effect leads to technological change favoring the abundant factor while the price effect encourages innovation toward the scarce factor, with such decisions made endogenously. The elasticity of substitution measures the market and price effects strength with technological change and factor prices interacting with changes in relative supply.

With Acemoglu (2002) notation:

$$\sigma_{ZL} = \frac{dz}{d\omega}\frac{\omega}{z} > 1 \xrightarrow{yields} \frac{dz}{z} > \frac{d\omega}{\omega} \xrightarrow{yields} \frac{d\left(\frac{Z}{L}\right)}{Z/L} > \frac{d\left(\frac{w_L}{w_Z}\right)}{w_L/w_Z} \tag{E.1}$$

where $z = Z/L$ and $\omega = w_L/w_z$. With $\sigma > 1$, factor shares are very responsive to changes in relative factor prices.

Notwithstanding a 30-year gap in the literature and a lack of microfoundations, Acemoglu (2002) cites the early work of Kennedy (1964) and Habakkuk (1962) who hypothesized labor scarcity and with increasing wages, induced firms to search to labor-saving innovations and spurred technological progress.

To explore in more detail, equation E.2 specifies a constant elasticity of substitution production function:

$$y = \left[\gamma\left(A_L L\right)^{\frac{\sigma-1}{\sigma}} + \left(1-\gamma\right)\left(A_Z Z\right)^{\frac{\sigma-1}{\sigma}}\right]^{\frac{\sigma}{\sigma-1}} \tag{E.2}$$

where A_Z and A_L are technology indices. An increase in A corresponds to "better technology." Z can be capital, high-skill labor, unskilled labor, or some other factor.

Whether technological change is labor-biased or Z-biased depends on the elasticity of substitution. To see this, from (E.2) calculate the relative marginal product of the factors:

$$\frac{MP_Z}{MP_L} = \frac{1-\gamma}{\gamma} \left(\frac{A_Z}{A_L} \right)^{\frac{\sigma-1}{\sigma}} \left(\frac{Z}{L} \right)^{-\frac{1}{\sigma}} \tag{E.3}$$

The relative marginal product of Z is decreasing in Z and Z/L, which is a substitution effect resulting in a downward sloping demand curve. However, the effect of A_Z on the relative marginal product of Z, depends on whether σ is greater or less than one.

If $\sigma > 1$, an increase in A_Z relative to A_L increases the relative marginal product of Z. "Better technology," when the factors are gross substitutes, means Z-augmenting technology is also Z-biased.

If $\sigma < 1$, an increase in A_Z relative to A_L reduces the relative marginal product of Z. "Better technology," when the factors are gross complements, means Z-augmenting technology is L-biased. Intuitively, when $\sigma < 1$ with Z-augmenting technological change, an increase in the productivity of Z increases the demand for the other factor, labor. As a result, the marginal productivity of labor increases by more than the marginal product of Z.

With profit incentives determining the type and nature of technological and business innovation, A_Z and A_L are determined endogenously as a result of the quality of technology. Acemoglu (2002) shows that the profitability of new Z-complementary technology relative to the profitability of L-complementary technology is:

$$\Pi_Z = \phi \left(\frac{A_Z}{A_L} \right)^{\frac{-1}{\sigma}} \left(\frac{Z}{L} \right)^{\frac{\sigma-1}{\sigma}} \tag{E.4}$$

Π_Z is the Z-complementary technology profit relative to the L-complementary profit and ϕ is a proportionality factor. Taking the partial derivative of (E.4) with respect to Z/L yields:

$$\frac{\delta \Pi_Z}{\delta Z / L} = \frac{\sigma - 1}{\sigma} \phi \left(\frac{A_Z}{A_L} \frac{Z}{L} \right)^{\frac{-1}{\sigma}} \tag{E.5}$$

If $\sigma > 1$, then

$$\frac{\delta \Pi_Z}{\delta Z / L} > 0$$

If $\sigma < 1$, then

$$\frac{\delta \Pi_Z}{\delta Z / L} < 0$$

If the factors are gross substitutes, $\sigma > 1$, an increase in Z/L will increase the relative profitability of Z-complementary innovation. For equilibrium, A_Z/A_L has to increase, incenting the development of "better technology" and reducing Π_Z to its original level. When the elasticity of substitution is high, $\sigma > 1$, abundant factors create a force toward innovation, and the market effect is relatively more powerful. The market size effect encourages the development of technologies that have a larger market with technologies using the more abundant factor.

If the factors are gross complements, $\sigma < 1$, an increase in Z/L will decrease the relative profitability of Z-complementary innovation, calling forth more or better-quality L, providing improved earnings, and resulting in a fall in A_Z/A_L. While the increase in L reduces the relative physical productivity of factor Z, relative price changes increase the value of the marginal product of Z-complementary technology and its reward. When the elasticity of substitution is low, $\sigma < 1$, scarce factors command higher prices, and the price effect is relatively more powerful. The price effect creates incentives to develop technologies used in the production of more expensive goods with higher rewards earned by both Z and L.

As a result, whether the factors are gross substitutes, $\sigma > 1$, or gross complements, $\sigma < 1$, an increase in Z causes Z-biased technological change. However, the consequent demand for L will depend on whether $\sigma > 1$ or $\sigma < 1$. As Acemoglu observes, if σ is sufficiently large—on either side of one—the induced Z-biased technological change "can be so powerful that the increase in the relative abundance of a factor may in fact increase its relative reward" (Acemoglu 2002, 786).[1] As we have written in detail, innovation and creative destruction is a continuous, ongoing process. The factor in relative abundance with an increasing reward could

---

[1] The effect of induced Z-biased technology also required $\sigma \neq 1$.

be capital, high-skill labor, unskilled labor, or some other. The response of labor will depend—as indicated by σ—on the maturity of the technology, the age of the capital stock, and the diffusion of knowledge. The stage of the industrial revolution is a signal of the ability of labor to benefit.

Recent scholarship (see Rognlie 2015) as well as the original work of Hicks (1932) suggest that labor and capital shares net of depreciation are the appropriate measures. Solow (2015) observes "it becomes obvious that the return net of depreciation is what matters .... The only reason research has devoted so much effort to gross concepts was the sense that measured depreciation might verge on the meaningless because it reflected accounting conventions and tax incentives that had little to do changing productive capacity of plants and equipment."

Almost a century after Hicks, Karabarbounis, and Neiman (2014a and 2014b) revived the focus on measures net of depreciation as a potential explanation of the evidence presented for secular declines in the global labor share.

Based on cross-country variation and covering the period 1975 to 2012, Karabarbounis and Neiman present elasticity of substitution estimates of approximately $\sigma = 1.25$, suggesting for every 1 percent increase in the real wage rate relative to the real interest rate, the capital–labor ratio increased by 1.25 percent.[2] Capital is substituted for labor. However, the Karabarbounis and Neiman estimate covers only the installation period of the Fourth Industrial Revolution. As Rognlie (2015) observes:

> The net capital share generally fell from the beginning of the sample [1948] through the mid-1970s, at which point the trends reversed. In the long run, there is a moderate increase in the aggregate net capital share, but this owes entirely to the housing sector … Outside of housing, there is a pronounced U-shape in the net capital share, with a steep fall in the 1970s and a more recent recovery. (Rognlie 2015, 3)

Consistent with Rognlie's observed data, the current hypothesis is that values of the elasticity of substitution can vary over multidecade periods.

---

[2] Autor, Dorn, Katz, Patterson, and Van Reenen (2020) in footnote 2 caution of the difficulty in estimating the elasticity of substitution values.

Lacking detailed industry–country data for the period prior to 1975, as was available to Karabarbounis and Neiman, the calculation of the elasticity of substation is limited to the aggregate level—in this case, the United States. With Bureau of Economic Analysis chain-type quantity indexes for net stock of fixed private nonresidential assets available from 1925 to 2019 and Bureau of Labor Statistics nonfarm payroll employment, annual capital–labor ratios can be calculated. Figure E.1 shows substantial capital–labor ratio decline during the 1930s and 1940s followed by an extended period of rapid growth into the 21st century when some slowing appears. Figure E.2 shows the real hourly wage rate and the real rental rate of capital.

With the available data, the elasticity of substitution can be calculated over the 1945–1976 period and over the 1975–2019 period. For the 1945–1976 period, the Third Industrial Revolution's deployment period, the elasticity remains well below 1. With a value of $\sigma = 0.313$ in 1976, suggesting capital and labor complementary over the period. In 2010, $\sigma = 1.534$ suggesting capital and labor are substitutes in the Fourth Industrial Revolution's installation period.[3]

Figure E.1 U.S. capital–labor ratio

Source: For capital stock data: US Bureau of Economic Analysis. Fixed Assets Accounts Table. Table 1.2 Chain-type quantity indexes for net stock of fixed assets and consumer durable goods. For labor input data: Nonfarm payrolls, thousands of persons, annual, seasonally adjusted.

---

[3] That capital and labor have been asserted to be gross substitutes in the recent years, requires little documentation. The issue has been widely discussed. Basic business processes—human resources, finance, manufacturing, office support—have been highly automated.

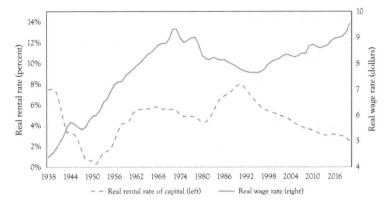

Figure E.2 U.S. real factor prices

Source: Real wage rate: U.S. Bureau of Labor Statistics, average hourly earnings of production and nonsupervisory employees: Total private and consumer price index of all urban consumers: all items. Real rental rate = $(\delta_t + r_t) * q_t/p_t$, where δ_t is the depreciation for period t, r_t is the real interest rate for period t, q_t is the price of the investment, and p_t is the general price index.

Data Source: U.S. Bureau of Economic Analysis, Fixed Assets Accounts Table, Table 1.3 Current-cost depreciation of fixed assets and consumer durable goods, nonresidential depreciation as a percent of stock; Baa Real Rates from Real Interest Rates Moody's Seasoned Baa Corporate Bond Yield; U.S. Bureau of Economic Analysis, national Income and Product Accounts; Table 1.1.4 Price indexers for nonresidential gross private domestic investment; and U.S. Bureau of Labor Statistics, consumer price index for all urban consumers: all items.

Notwithstanding the data limitations for the period prior to 1975, Knoblach and Stockl (2020) collect σ estimates from 853 estimates from 49 published studies covering the period from 1961 to 2017. Estimates range from zero to slightly above 1, with a peak between 0.9 and 1.0 with most estimates in the range of 0.3 to 0.7. Knoblach and Stockl make a number of observations focusing on the heterogeneity of estimates across industries and sectors. In addition, Knoblach and Stockl find "there is increasing evidence that the elasticity of substitution of the U.S. economy is rising" over the period (Knoblach and Stockl 2020, 852). While surely not definitive, some elasticity of substitution evidence suggests capital and labor complementary in the 1945–1976 period and substitutability over the 1975–2019 period.

Appendix F

Employee Trust and Productivity

To formalize the relationship between employee trust and productivity, Brown, Gray, McHardy, and Taylor (2015) propose a principal agent model. Assume the principal is risk-neutral, v is a vector of outcomes, p_a is a vector of probabilities, a is index of high-cost actions H or low-cost actions L.

The objective is to design a payment contract $w(v)$ to

$$\text{Maximize } (v - w)\, p_H \tag{F.1}$$

subject to the agent's incentive compatibility constraint:

$$u(w)\, p_H - c_H \geq u(w)\, p_L - c_L$$

and participation constraint is:

$$u(w)\, p_H - c_H \geq \bar{u}$$

where u is the agent's expected utility function and $u = u(w)\, p_a - c_a$. The agent is risk averse and $\bar{u}$ is the reservation utility.

Productivity improvement requires business process transformation which, in turn, requires work and task transformation. Suppose that, to achieve a new, more profitable, organizational regime, the principal wishes to uplift worker skills, reconfigure working practices or redesign the working environment.

The principal's objective is to design a reward profile $(w(s),\ e(s),\ w(n),\ e(n))$ where w is the wage, e is the working environment, s is the status quo, and n is the new regime to

$$\text{Maximize} \qquad\qquad \pi\left(w_n, e_n\right) \tag{F.2}$$

subject to an optimality constraint:

$$\pi_n\left(w_n, e_n\right) \geq \delta + \pi_s\left(w_s, e_s\right)$$

where δ is the time-adjusted value of the cost of the organizational change and/or training; and also subject to an agent-incentive compatibility constraint:

$$u\left(w_n, e_n\right) \geq w + u\left(w_s, e_s\right)$$

where w is the time-adjusted cost to the agent of the organizational change and/or training; and a participation constraint, with reservation utility, $\bar{u}$: $u\left(w_n, e_n\right) - w \geq \bar{u}$.

References

Abowd, J.M., F. Kramarz, and D.N. Margolis. 1999. "High Wage Workers and High Wage Firms." *Econometrica* 67, no. 2, pp. 251–333.

Acemoglu, D. 2002. "Directed Technical Change." *Review of Economic Studies* 69, pp. 781–809.

Acemoglu, D. 2020. *14.452 Economic Growth, Lecture 11, Directed Technological Change*. Fall.

Acemoglu, D., and P. Restrepo. 2019. "Automation and New Tasks: How Technology Displaces and Reinstates Labor." *Journal of Economic Perspectives* 33, no. 2, pp. 3–30.

Acemoglu, D., and P. Restrepo. 2020. "Robots and Jobs: Evidence From U.S. Labor markets." *Journal of Political Economy* 128, no. 6.

Acemoglu, D., A. Manera, and P. Restrepo. 2020. "Does the U.S. Tax Code Favor Automation?" *Brookings Papers on Economic Activity*, Spring, pp. 231–300.

Acemoglu, D., D. Autor, J. Hazell, and P. Restrepo. January 03, 2021. "AI and Jobs: Evidence from Online Vacancies." Paper presented at the American Economic Association 2021 Annual Meeting.

Aghion, P., C. Antonin, and S. Bunel. 2021. *The Power of Creative Destruction, Economic Upheaval and the Wealth of Nations*. Cambridge: The Belknap Press.

Akcigit, U., and S.T. Ates. August 27, 2020. "Slowing Business Dynamism and Productivity Growth in the United States." Federal Reserve Bank of Kansas City, Jackson Hole Symposium 2020.

Akcigit, U., and S.T. Ates. 2021. "Ten Facts on Declining Business Dynamics and Lesson from Endogenous Growth Theory." *American Economic Journal: Macroeconomics* 13, no. 1, pp. 257–298.

Albaz, A., M. Dondi, T. Rida, and J. Schubert. June 2020. *Unlocking Growth in Small and Medium-Size Enterprises*. McKinsey Global Institute.

Aliber, R.Z., and C.P. Kindleberger. 2015. *Manias, Panics and Crashes, A History of Financial Crises*, Seventh Edition. New York, NY: Palgrave Macmillan.

Allas, T., and B. Schaninger. 2020. *The Boss Factor: Making the World a Better Place Through Workplace Relationships*. McKinsey Global Institute.

Allen, R.C. 1983. "Collective Invention." *Journal of Economic Behavior and Organization* 4, no. 1, pp. 1–24.

Allen, R.C. 2009. "Engels' Pause: Technical Change, Capital Accumulation, and Inequality in the British Industrial Revolution." *Explorations in Economic History* 46, no. 4, pp. 418–435.

Allen, R.C. May 2017. "Class Structure and Inequality during the Industrial Revolution: Lessons from England's Social Tables, 1688-1867." Working Paper # 0002.

Andrews, D., C. Criscuolo, and P.N. Gal. 2016. "The Best Versus the Rest: The Global Productivity Slowdown, Divergence across Firms and the Role of Public Policy." OECD Productivity Working Papers, 2016-05, OECD Publishing, Paris.

Ardanaz-Badia, A, G. Awano, and P. Wales. April 2017a. "Labour Productivity Measures From the Annual Business Survey: 2006 to 2015." Office of National Statistics.

Ardanaz-Badia, A., G. Awano, and P. Wales. July 2017b. "Understanding Firms in the Bottom 10% of the Labour Productivity Distribution in Great Britain: 'The Laggards', 2003 to 2015." Office of National Statistics.

Arthur, W.B. 2021. "Foundations of Complexity Economics." *Nature Reviews Physics* 3, pp. 136–145.

Autor, D., D. Dorn, L.F. Katz, C. Patterson, and J.V. Reenen. 2020. "The Fall of the Labor Share and the Rise of Superstar Firms." *The Quarterly Journal of Economics*, pp. 645–709.

Baily, M.N. 1981. "Productivity and the Services of Capital and Labor." *Brookings Papers on Economic Activity*, no. 1, pp. 1–65.

Baldwin R. 2016. "The Great Convergence: Information Technology and the New Globalization." Cambridge: Harvard University Press.

Baldwin R., J.I. Haaland, and A. Venables. January 2021. *Jobs and Technology in General Equilibrium: A Three Elasticities Approach*. London: Centre for Economic Policy Research, Discussion Paper DP 15739.

Banerjee, A.V., and D. Esther. 2019. *Good Economics for Hard Times*. Ney York, NY: Hachette Book Group, Inc.

Barrero, J.M., N. Bloom, and S.J. Davis. April 2021. "Why Working from Home Will Stick." National Bureau of Economic Research, Working Paper 28731.

Bellet, C.S., J.E. De Neve, and G. Ward. February 08, 2020. "Does Employee Happiness Have an Impact on Productivity?" https://ssrn.com/abstract=3470734

Berlingieri, G., S. Calligaris, and C. Criscuolo. 2018. "The Productivity-Wage Premium: Does Size Still Matter in a Service Economy?" *American Economic Association Papers and Proceedings* 108, pp. 328–333.

Berlingieri, G., S. Calligaris, C. Criscuolo, and R. Verlhac. 2020. *Laggard Firms, Technology Diffusion and Its Structural and Policy Determinants*. OECD Science, Technology and Industry Policy Papers, no. 86.

Bessen, J., and A. Nuvolari. 2016. "Knowledge Sharing Among Inventors: Some Historical Perspectives." In D. Harhoff and K.R. Lakhani, *Revolutionizing Innovation: Users, Communities, and Open Innovation*. Cambridge, MA: The MIT Press.

Betti, F., E. de Boer, and Y. Giraud. 2020. *The Fourth Industrial Revolution and Manufacturing's Great Reset*. McKinsey Global Institute.

Bessen, J. 2003. "Technology and Learning by Factory Workers: The Stretch-out at Lowell, 1842." *The Journal of Economic History* 63, no. 1, pp. 33–64.

Bessen, J. 2015. *Learning by Doing; The Real Connection between Innovation Wages, and Wealth*. New Haven, Yale: University Press.

Blanchard, O.J., and L.H. Summers. June 1986. *Hysteresis and the European Unemployment Problem*. National Bureau of Economic Research, Working Paper No. 1950.

Blanchard, O.J., E. Cerutti, and L.H. Summers. November 2014. *Inflation and Activity—Two Explorations and their Monetary Policy Implications*. IMF Working Paper, Research Department.

Bloom, N., and J.V. Reenen. 2007. "Measuring and Explaining Management Practices Across Firms and Countries." *The Quarterly Journal of Economics* 122, no. 4, pp. 1351–1408.

Bloom, N., B. Eifert, A. Mahajan, D. McKenzie, and J. Roberts. 2013. "Does Management Matter? Evidence from India." *Quarterly Journal of Economics* 128, no. 1, pp. 1–51.

Bloom, N., E. Brynjolfsson, L. Foster, R. Jarmin, M. Patnaik, I. Saporta-Eksten, and J.V Reenen. 2019. "What Drives Differences in Management Practices?" *American Economic Review* 109, no. 5, pp. 1648–1683.

Bloom, N., R. Sadun, and J.V. Reenen. 2012. "Americans Do IT Better: U.S. Multinationals and the Productivity Miracle." *American Economic Review* 102, no. 1, pp. 167–2011.

Bloom, N., T.A. Hassan, A. Kalyani, J. Lerner, and A. Tahoun. July 2021. "The Diffusion of Disruptive Technologies." National Bureau of Economic Research, Working Paper 28999.

Bolt, J., and J.L. Van Zanden. October 2020. *Maddison Style Estimates of the Evolution of the World Economy, A New 2020 Update*.

Bresnahan, T. May 2019. *Artificial Intelligence Technologies and Aggregate Growth Prospects*. Version IV.

Brey, B. November 2021. *The Long-Run Gains from the Early Adoption of Electricity*. Université Libre de Bruxelles (ECARES).

Broadberry, S. 1997. *The Productivity Race: British Manufacturing in International Perspective, 1850–1990*. Cambridge, U.K.: Cambridge University Press.

Broadberry, S., B.M.S. Campbell, A. Klein, M. Overton, and B.V. Leeuwen. 2015. *British Economic Growth, 1270-1870*, Cambridge, U.K.: Cambridge University Press.

Brown, S., D. Gray, J. McHardy, and K. Taylor. 2015. "Employee Trust and Workplace Performance." *Journal of Economic Behavior & Organization* 116, pp. 361–378.

Bryl, Ł. 2018. "Human Capital Orientation and Financial Performance: A Comparative Analysis of US Corporations." *Journal of Entrepreneurship, Management and Innovation* 14, no. 3, pp. 61–86.

Brynjolfsson, E. 2022. "The Turing Trap: The Promise & Peril of Human-Like Artificial Intelligence." *Dædalus,* Spring.

Brynjolfsson, E., A. McAfee, M. Sorell, and F. Zhu. 2008. "Scale Without Mass: Business Process Replication and Industry Dynamics." Harvard Business School Working Paper 07-016.

Brynjolfsson, E., D. Rock, and C. Syverson. 2021. "The Productivity J-Curve: How Intangibles Complement General Purpose Technologies." *American Economic Journal: Macroeconomics* 13, no. 1, pp. 333–372.

Bryson, A. May 2017. "Does Employees' Subjective Well-Being Affect Workplace Performance." *Human Relations.*

Buehler, K., R. Dooley, L. Grennan, and A. Singla. May 2021. *Getting to Know— And Manage—Your Biggest AI Risks.* McKinsey & Company.

Caballero, R. 2010. "Creative Destruction." In S.N. Durlauf and L.E. Blume, *Economic Growth,* pp. 24–29. Germany: SpringerLink, Berlin/Heidelberg.

Carney, M. September 14, 2018. *The Future of Work.* 2018 Whitaker Lecture. Central Bank of Ireland.

Chandler, A.D., Jr. 1998. "Creating Competitive Capability: Innovation and Investment in the United States, Great Britain, and Germany from the 1870s to World War I." In P. Higonnet, D.S. Landes, H. Rosovsky, eds. *Favorites of Fortune: Technology, Growth, and Economic Development Since the Industrial Revolution.* Harvard University Press; Revised Edition.

Cohen, W.M., and D.A. Levinthal. 1990. "Absorptive Capacity: A New Perspective on Learning and Innovation." *Administrative Sciences Quarterly* 35, pp. 128–152.

Corrado, C. 2023 Forthcoming. "Measuring Intangibles." In L. Sheiner and M. Reinsdorf, eds. *Measuring the Hard-to-Measure in a Changing Economy.* Chicago: University of Chicago Press.

Coyle, D. June 2021. "The Idea of Productivity." The Productivity Institute Working Paper 003.

Crafts, N., and C.K. Harley. 1992. "Output Growth and the British Industrial Revolution: A Restatement of the Crafts-Harley View." *Economic History Review* 45, no 4, p.703.

Crafts, N. 2004. "Steam as a General-Purpose Technology: A Growth Accounting Perspective." *Economic Journal* 114, no. 495, pp. 338–351.

Crafts, N. 2019. "The Sources of British Economic Growth since the Industrial Revolution: Not the Same Old Story." The Warwick Economics Research Paper Series (TWERPS) 1216, University of Warwick, Department of Economics.

Crafts, N. 2021a. "Understanding Productivity Growth in the Industrial Revolution." *Economic History Review* 74, no. 20, pp. 309–338.

Crafts, N. February 2021b. "Artificial Intelligence as General-Purpose Technology: An Historical Perspective." Working Paper.

Crafts, N. January 2002. *The Solow Productivity Paradox in Historical Perspective.* Center for Economic Policy Research, Discussion Paper No. 3142.

Crafts, N., and Mills, T.C. 2020a. "Sooner Than You Think; the Pre-1914 U.K. Productivity Slowdown Was Victorian Not Edwardian." *European Review of Economic History* 24, no. 4, pp. 736–748.

Crafts, N., and Mills, T.C. 2020b. 'The Race Between Population and Technology: Real Wages in the First Industrial Revolution." *Centre for Economic Policy Research.* Discussion Paper No. 15174.

Crouzet, N., and J. Eberly. March 2020. *Rents and Intangible Capital: AQ+ Framework.*

Cullenberg, S.E., and I. Dasgupta. 2001. "From Myth to Metaphor: A Semiological Analysis of the Cambridge Capital Controversy." In J. Amariglio, S.E Cullenberg, and D.F Ruccio ed. *Postmodernism, Economics and Knowledge* 1st Edition, Chapter 16, pp. 337–353. Routledge.

David, P.A. 1990. "The Dynamo and the Computer: An Historical Perspective on the Modern Productivity Paradox." *American Economic Review, Papers and Proceedings* 80, no. 2, pp. 355–361.

David, P.A. 1998. "The Hero and the Herd in Technology History: Reflections on Thomas Edison and the Battle of the Systems." In P. Higonnet, D.S. Landes, H. Rosovsky, eds. *Favorites of Fortune: Technology, Growth, and Economic Development Since the Industrial Revolution.* Harvard University Press; Revised Edition.

Denison, E. 1985. *Trends in American Economic Growth.* Washington, DC: Brookings Institution Press.

Dickens, C. 1837. *The Pickwick Papers.* Chapman & Hall, Serialized March 1836–November 1837; book format 1837.

Dickens, C. 1842. *A Christian Carol.* Chapman & Hall, 1843.

Dickens, C. 1842. *American Notes for General Circulation.* Chapman & Hall, 1842.

Dieppe, A. 2020. *Global Productivity: Trends, Drivers, and Policies.* Washington, DC: World Bank.

Dustmann, C., A. Lindner, U. Schönberg, M. Umkehrer, and P. vom Berge 2020. "Reallocation Effects of the Minimum Wage." *The Quarterly Journal of Economics* 137, no. 1, February 2022, pp. 267–328.

Easterly, W. 2001. *The Elusive Quest for Growth.* Cambridge, MA: MIT Press.

Eichengreen, B. 2015. "Secular Stagnation: The Long View." *American Economic Review* 105, no. 5, pp. 66–70.

Elsby, M.W.L., B. Hobijn, and A. Sahin. 2013. "The Decline of the U.S. Labor Share." *Brookings Papers on Economic Activity* 2, pp. 1–63.

European Investment Bank. 2022. *Recovery as a Springboard for Change.* Luxembourg: European Investment Bank.

Faria e Castro, M. 2021. "The COVID Retirement Boom." *Economic Synopsis.* Federal Reserve Bank of St. Louis, no. 25.

Fernald, J.G. 2016. "Reassessing Longer-Run U.S. Growth: How Low?" Federal Reserve Bank of San Francisco Working Paper 2016-18. www.frbsf.org/economic-research/publications/working-papers/wp2016-18.pdf

Fernald, J.G. 2019. "A Quarterly, Utilization-Adjusted Series on Total Factor Productivity." *FRBSF Working Paper* 2012–19.

Fisman, R., and M. Luca. January 23, 2021. "How Higher Wages Can Increase Profits." *Wall Street Journal*, p. C3.

Fleming, M. 2021. *Productivity Growth and Capital Deepening in the Fourth Industrial Revolution*. Working Paper No. 010, The Productivity Institute.

Forrester, J. August 13, 1981. "Innovation and Economic Change." *Futures*, pp. 323–331.

Foster, L., J. Haltiwanger, and C.J. Krizan. 2001. "Aggregate Productivity Growth: Lessons from Microeconomic Evidence." In *New Developments in Productivity Analysis*, ed. C.R. Hulten, E.R. Dean, and M.J. Harper, pp. 303–363. Chicago and London: University of Chicago Press.

Foster, L., J. Haltiwanger, and C. Syverson. 2008. "Reallocation, Firm Turnover, and Efficiency: Selection on Productivity or Profitability?" *American Economic Review* 98, no. 1, pp. 394–425.

Freeman, C., J. Clark, and L. Soete. 1982 *Unemployment and Technical Innovation: A Study of Long Waves and Economic Development*. London: Frances Pinter.

Fries, S. 2021. Transforming Energy Systems; Economics, Policies and Change. Cheltenham, U.K.: Edward Elgar Publishing.

Furman, J., and L. Summers. December 2020. *A Reconsideration of Fiscal Policy in the Era of Low Interest Rates*. Paper prepared for presentation to the Hutchins Center on Fiscal & Monetary Policy and Peterson Institute for International Economics.

Garten, J.E. 2021. *Three Days at Camp David*. New York, NY: HarperCollins Publishers.

Geels, F.W., J. Pinkse, and D. Zenghelis. 2021. "Productivity Opportunities and Risks in a Transformative, Low-Carbon and Digital Age." Working Paper No. 009, The Productivity Institute.

Gilchrist, D.S., M. Luca, and D. Malhotra. 2016. "When 3+1>4: Gift Structure and Reciprocity in the Field." *Management Science* 62, no. 9.

Gilchrist, S., and J.C. Williams. May 2002. *Investment, Capacity, and Uncertainty: A Putty-Clay Approach*. Federal Reserve Bank of San Francisco Working Paper 2002-3, San Francisco CA.

Goldschmidt, D., and J.F. Schmieder. 2017. "The Rise of Domestic Outsourcing and the Evolution of the German Wage Structure." *Quarterly Journal of Economics* 132, no. 3, pp. 1165–1217.

Goodhart, C., and M. Pradhan. 2020. *The Great Demographic Reversal*. London: Palgrave Macmillan.

Gordon, R.J. 2016. *The Rise and Fall of American Growth: The U.S. Standard of Living since the Civil War.* Princeton, NJ: Princeton University Press.

Greenspan, A. April 27, 2001. *The Paydown of Federal Debt.* Remarks before the Bond Market Association, White Sulphur Springs, West Virginia.

Greenspan, A. December 19, 2002. *Issues for Monetary Policy.* Remarks before the Economic Club of New York, New York City.

Habakkuk, H.J. 1962. *American and British Technology in the Nineteenth Century: Search for Labor Saving Inventions.* Cambridge, U.K.: Cambridge University Press.

Haltiwanger, J.C. June 2021. *Entrepreneurship During the COVID-19 Pandemic: Evidence from the Business Formation Statistics.* NBER Working Paper No. 28912.

Hamilton, J.D. 2017. "Why You Should Never Use the Hodrick-Prescott Filter." Working Paper.

Hansen, A.H. March 1939. "Economic Progress and Declining Population Growth." *American Economic Review* 29, no. 1, pp. 1–15.

Harberger, A.C. 1998. "A Vision of the Growth Process." *American Economic Review* 88, no. 1, pp. 1–31.

Harter, J.K., F.L. Schmidt, and T.L. Hayes. 2002. "Business-Unit-Level Relationship Between Employee Satisfaction, Employee Engagement, and Business Outcomes: A Meta-Analysis." *Journal of Applied Psychology* 87, no. 2, pp. 268–279.

Haskel, J., and S. Westlake. 2018. *Capitalism Without Capital.* Princeton: Princeton University Press.

Hercowitz, Z. 1998. "The 'Embodiment' Controversy: A Review Essay." *Journal of Monetary Economics* 41, pp. 217–224.

Hershbein, B., and H. Holzer. 2021. "The Covid-19 Pandemic's Evolving Impact on the Labor Market: Who Has Been Hurt and What Should We Do." IZA Discussion Paper.

Heskett, J.L., W.E. Sasser Jr., and L.A. Schlesinger. 2015. *What Great Service Leaders Know and Do: Creating Breakthroughs in Service Firms.* Oakland: Berrett-Koehler Publishers.

Hicks, J. 1932. *The Theory of Wages.* New York, NY: Palgrave Macmillan.

Hodrick, R., and E.C. Prescott. 1997. "Postwar U.S. Business Cycles: An Empirical Investigation." *Journal of Money, Credit, and Banking* 29, no. 1, pp. 1–16. JSTOR 2953682.

Hodrick, R.J. 2020. "An Exploration of Trend-Cycle Decomposition Methodologies in Simulated Data." Working Paper.

Holzer, H.J. May 2019. "The US Labor Market in 2050: Supply, Demand and Policies to Improve Outcomes." IZA Institute of Labor Economics Policy Paper No. 148.

Hotchkiss, J. 2022. *Will Wage Growth Alone Get Workers Back into the Labor Market? Not Likely.* Federal Reserve Bank of Atlanta Working Paper No. 2022-2.

Hulten, C.R. 2001. "Total Factor Productivity: A Short Biography." In *New Developments in Productivity Analysis*, ed. C.R. Hulten, E.R. Dean, and M.J. Harper, pp 1–54. Chicago and London: University of Chicago Press.

IBM Institute of Business Value. 2020. *The Business Value of AI.* Armonk, NY: IBM.

Janeway, W.H. 2012. "Doing Capitalism in the Innovation Economy." U.K.: Cambridge University Press.

Johansen, L. 1959. "Substitution Versus Fixed Production Coefficients in the Theory of Economic Growth: A Synthesis." *Econometrica* 27, no. 2, pp. 157–176. JSTOR 1909440.

Jordà, Ò., S.R. Singh, and A.M. Taylor. June 2020. *Longer-Run Economic Consequences of Pandemics.* NBER Working Paper No. 26934.

Jorgenson, D.W., M.S. Ho, and J.D. Samuels. 2019. "Educational Attainment and the Revival of U.S. Economic Growth." In *Education, Skills, and Technical Change: Implications for Future U.S. GDP Growth*, C.R. Hulten and V.A. Ramey, ed., pp. 23–60. Chicago: University of Chicago Press.

Jorgenson, D., and K.J. Stiroh. 2000. "Raising the Speed Limit: U.S. Economic Growth in the Information Age." *Brookings Papers on Economic Activity* 1, pp. 125–212.

Kaldor, N. 1961. "Capital Accumulation and Economic Growth." In *The Theory of Capital*, ed. F.A. Lutz and D.C. Hague, pp. 177–222, New York, NY: St. Martin's Press.

Karabarbounis, L., and B. Neiman. 2014a. "The Global Decline of the Labor Share." *Quarterly Journal of Economics* 129, no. 1, pp. 61–103.

Karabarbounis, L., and B. Neiman. 2014b. *Capital Depreciation and Labor Shares around the World: Measurement and Implications.* NBER Working Paper No. 20606. Cambridge, Mass.

Kaur, S., S. Mullainathan, S. Oh, and F. Schilbach. January 2021. *Do Financial Concerns Make Workers Less Productive?* NBER Working Paper No. 28338.

Kelly, B., D. Papanikolaou, A. Seru, and M. Taddy. 2021. "Measuring Technological Innovation over the Long Run." *American Economic Review: Insights* 3, no. 3, pp. 303–320.

Kendrick, J.W. 1961. *Productivity Trends in the United States.* Cambridge, Ma: National Bureau of Economic Research.

Kennedy, C. 1964. "Induced Bias in Innovation and the Theory of Distribution." *Economic Journal*, LXXIV, pp. 541–547.

Keshavarzi Arshadi A., J. Webb, M. Salem, E. Cruz, S. Calad-Thomson, N. Ghadirian, J. Collins, E. Diez-Cecilia, B. Kelly, H. Goodarzi, and J.S. Yuan. 2020. "Artificial Intelligence for COVID-19 Drug Discovery and

Vaccine Development." *Frontiers in Artificial Intelligence* 3, p. 65. https://doi.org/10.3389/frai.2020.00065

Knoblach, M., and F. Stockl. 2020. "What Determines the Elasticity of Substitution Between Capital and Labor? A Literature Review." *Journal of Economic Surveys* 34, no. 4, pp. 847–875.

Kondratiev, N. 1979. "The Long Waves in Economic Life." *Review* 4, pp. 519–562; A complete translation of "The Major Economic Cycles." 1925. *Voprosy Koniunktury* 1, pp. 28–79.

Kuznets, S. 1955. "Economic Growth and Income Inequality." *American Economic Review* 45, no. 1, pp. 1–28.

Landes, D.S. 1969. *The Unbounded Prometheus; Technological Change and Industrial Development in Western Europe from 1750 to the Present*. Cambridge, U.K.: Cambridge University Press, Second Edition, 2008.

Lasky, M. September 2003. *A Putty-Clay Model of Business Fixed Investment*, Congressional Budget Office Working Paper 2003-9, Washington, DC.

Lazonick, W. 1998. "What Happened to the Theory of Economic Development?" In P. Higonnet, D.S. Landes, H. Rosovsky, eds. *Favorites of Fortune: Technology, Growth, and Economic Development Since the Industrial Revolution*. Harvard University Press; Revised Edition.

Lee, K.F. 2018. *AI Superpowers; China, Silicon Valley and the New World Order*. Boston, MA: Houghton Mifflin Harcourt.

Levy, F., and P. Temin. 2007. "Inequality and Institutions in 20th Century America." Industrial Performance Center, Massachusetts Institute of Technology, MIT-IPC-07-002.

Lewis, W.A. May 1954. "Economic Development with Unlimited Supplies of Labour." *Manchester School of Economics and Social Studies* 22, pp. 139–191.

Liu, Z., J. Fernald, and S. Basu. 2012. "Technology Shocks in a Two-Sector DSGE Model." 2012 Meeting Papers 1017, Society for Economic Dynamics.

Long, H. January 09, 2022. "Why Manufacturing Workers Are Voluntarily Leaving Jobs At Rates Never Seen Before." *Washington Post*.

Lucas, R. 1988. "On the Mechanics of Economic Development." *Journal of Monetary Economics* 22, no. 1, pp. 3–42.

Ma, S. 2021. "Technology Obsolescence." Yale University School of Management.

Maddison, A. 1979. "Per Capita Output in the Long Run." *Kyklos* 32, no. (1 and 2), pp. 412–429.

Maddison, A. 1982. "Phases of Capitalist Development." New York, NY: Oxford University Press.

Maddison, A. 1991. Dynamic Forces in Capitalist Development. New York, NY: Oxford University Press.

Malthus, T. 1798. *An Essay on the Principle of Population*. (W. Pickering, London, 1986).

Manyika, J., A. Madgavkar, T. Tacke, J. Woetzel, S. Smit, and A. Abdulaal. February 2020. *The Social Contract in the 21st Century; Outcomes So Far for Workers, Consumers, and Savers in Advanced Economies.* McKinsey Global Institute.

Mas, A. 2008. "Labour Unrest and the Quality of Production: Evidence from the Construction Equipment Resale Market." *Review of Economic Studies* 75, no. 1, pp. 229–258.

Mazzucato, M. 2021. *Mission Economy, A Moonshot Guide to Changing Capitalism.* London: Alen Lane.

McAfee, A., and E. Brynjolfsson. 2017. *Machine, Platform, Crowd: Harnessing Our Digital Future.* W.W. Norton and Co. New York.

McKinsey Global Institute. January 2022. *The Net-Zero Transition; What It Would Cost, What It Could Bring.* New York, NY: McKinsey & Company.

Minsky, H.P. 1975. *John Maynard Keynes.* New York, NY: Columbia University Press.

Minsky, H.P. 1986. *Stabilizing an Unstable Economy.* Twentieth Century Fund Report. New Haven CT: Yale University Press.

Mokyr, J. 1990. *The Levers of Riches: Technical Creativity and Economic Progress.* New York, NY: Oxford University Press.

Mokyr, J. 1998. *The Second Industrial Revolution, 1870–1914.* Northwestern University.

Mokyr, J. 2011. *The Economics of the Industrial Revolution.* London: Routledge.

Mokyr, J. 2018. *A Culture of Growth: The Origins of the Modern Economy.* Princeton, NJ: Princeton University Press.

Nordhaus, W.D. 1997. "Do Real Output and Real Wages Capture Reality? The History of Light Suggests Not." In R.J. Gordon and T.F. Bresnahan, eds. *The Economics of New Goods*, pp. 29–66. Chicago, IL: University of Chicago Press.

Nordhaus, W.D. 2021. "Are We Approaching and Economic Singularity? Information Technology and the Future of Economic Growth." *American Economic Journal: Macroeconomics* 13, no. 10, pp. 299–332.

Nunn, N. 2021. "History as Evolution." In A. Bisin and G. Federico eds. *Handbook of Historical Economics.* Cambridge, MA: Academic Press.

OECD. 2015. *Taxation of SMEs in OECD and G20 Countries.* OECD Tax Policy Studies, No. 23, OECD Publishing, Paris.

OECD. 2021. *The Digital Transformation of SMEs.* OECD Studies on SMEs and Entrepreneurship, OECD Publishing, Paris.

Perez, C. 2002. *Technological Revolutions and Financial Capital.* U.K.: Edward Elgar, Cheltenham.

Posen, A.S. May/June 2021. "The Price of Nostalgia; America's Self-Defeating Economic Retreat." *Foreign Affairs*, pp. 28–43.

PWC. 2021. *PwC U.S. Pulse Survey: Next in Work; At a Pivotal Monet for the Future of Work, Companies Can Help Their Businesses and Employees Thrive.*

Rachel, L., and L.H. Summers. 2019. "On Secular Stagnation in the Industrialized World." *Brookings Papers on Economic Activity*, Spring, pp. 1–76.

Reinhart, C.M., and K.S. Rogoff. 2009. *This Time is Different, Eight Centuries of Financial Folly.* Princeton, NJ: Princeton University Press.

Ricardo, D. 1817. *On the Principles of Political Economy and Taxation.* Cambridge, U.K.: Cambridge University Press, 1951.

Rognlie, M. 2015. "Deciphering the Fall and Rise in the Net Capital Share: Accumulation or Scarcity?" *Brookings Papers on Economic Activity* 1, pp. 1–69.

Romer, P.M. 1986. "Increasing Returns and Long-Run Growth." *Journal of Political Economy* 94, no. 5, pp. 1002–1037.

Romer, P.M. 1987a. "Growth Based on Increasing Returns Due to Specialization." *American Economic Review, Papers and Proceedings* 77, no. 2, pp. 56–62.

Romer, P.M. 1987b. "Crazy Explanations for the Productivity Slowdown." In S. Fischer ed. *NBER Macroeconomics Annual* 2, pp. 163–210.

Romer, P.M. 1990. "Endogenous Technological Change." *Journal of Political Economy* 98, no. 5, pp. S71–S102.

Romer, P.M. 1993. "Two Strategies for Economic Development: Using Ideas and Producing Ideas." In *Proceedings of the World Bank Annual Conference of Development Economics 1992.* Washington, DC: World Bank.

Rosenberg, N., and C.R. Frischtak. 1983. "Long Waves and Economic Growth: A Critical Appraisal." *American Economic Association Papers and Proceedings* 73, no. 2, pp. 146–151.

Rostow, W.W. 1960. *Stages of Economic Growth, A Non-Communist Manifesto.* Cambridge, UK: Cambridge University Press.

Royal Swedish Academy of Sciences. 2018. *Economic Growth, Technology Change and Climate Change.* Scientific Background on the Sveriges Riksbank Prize in Economic Sciences in Memory of Alfred Nobel.

Ruffini, K. June 2020. *Worker Earnings, Service Quality, and Firm Profitability: Evidence from Nursing Homes and Minimum Wage Reforms.* Working Paper Series, Washington Center for Equitable Growth, 1156 15th St NW, Suite 700, Washington DC 2005.

Saez, E., and G. Zucman. October 2020. *Trends in U.S. Income and Wealth Inequality: Revising After the Revisionists.* NBER Working Paper 27921.

Schumpeter, J. 1939. *Business Cycles, A Theoretical, Historical and Statistical Analysis of the Capitalist Process.* New York, NY: McGraw–Hill.

Schumpeter, J.A. 1950. *Capitalism, Socialism and Democracy.* New York, NY: Harper Collins, 3rd edition 2008.

Schwab, K. 2016. *The Fourth Industrial Revolution.* Geneva: World Economic Forum.

Shafik, M. 2021. *What We Owe Each Other; A New Social Contract.* London: Bodley Head.

Shafik, N. December 2018. "A New Social Contract; Overcoming Fears of Technology and Globalization Means Rethinking the Rights and Obligations of Citizenship." *International Monetary Fund, Finance & Development* 55, no. 4.

Smith, A. 1776. *An Inquiry into the Nature and Causes of the Wealth of Nations.* (Random House, New York, 1937).

Solow, R.M. 1956. "A Contribution to the Theory of Economic Growth." *Quarterly Journal of Economics* 70, no. 1, pp. 65–94.

Solow, R.M. 2015. Comment on Matthew Rognlie, "Deciphering the Fall and Rise in the Net Capital Share: Accumulation or Scarcity?" *Brookings Papers on Economic Activity* 1, pp. 59–65.

Stansbury, A., and L.H. Summers. 2020. "Declining Worker Power and American Economic Performance." *Brookings Papers on Economic Activity,* Forthcoming.

Strauss, W., and N. Howe. 1997. *The Fourth Turning: An American Prophecy— What the Cycles of History Tell Us About America's Next Rendezvous with Destiny.* New York, NY: Penguin Random House.

Summers, L.H. 2014. "U.S. Economic Prospects: Secular Stagnation, Hysteresis, and the Zero Lower Bound." *Business Economics* 49, no. 2, pp. 65–73.

Summers, L.H. 2022. "Secular Stagnation and Post Pandemic Marco Economic Policy." comments presented on panel "Will U.S. Growth Be Higher than in Previous Decade after Pandemic Fiscal Stimulus Ends?" at American Economic Association Annual Meeting January.

Summers, R., and A. Heston. June 1984. "Improved International Comparisons of Real Product and its Composition: 1950–1980." *Review of Income and Wealth,* pp. 207–262.

Swan, T. December 1956. "Economic Growth and Capital Accumulation." *Economic Record* 32, pp. 334–361.

Syverson, C. 2011. "What Determines Productivity?" *Journal of Economic Literature* 49, no. 2, pp. 326–365.

The Economist. December 12, 2020. "Reasons to be Cheerful." pp. 69–71.

Tilly, R.H., and M.Kopsidis. 2020. *From Old Regime to Industrial State; A History of Germain Industrialization From the Eighteenth Century to World War I.* Chicago: University of Chicago Press.

van Ark, B., and A. Venables. 2020. "A Concerted Effort to Tackle the U.K. Productivity Puzzle." *International Productivity Monitor.* Centre for the Study of Living Standards, vol. 39, pp. 3–15, Fall.

van Ark, B., K. de Vries, and A. Erumban. 2020. *How to Not Miss a Productivity Revival Once Again?* National Institute of Economic and Social Research Discussion Paper No. 518.

van Ark, B., M. O'Mahony, and M.P. Timmer. 2008. "The Productivity Gap between Europe and the United States: Trends and Causes." *Journal of Economic Perspectives* 22, no. 1, pp. 25–44.

Van Reenen, J. May 2018. *Business Productivity Review.* Centre for Economic Performance, London School of Economics and Political Science.

Weinstein, E. January 06, 2022. "Beijing's 'Re-Innovation' Strategy Is Key Element of U.S.-China Competition." *Tech Stream.* Brookings Institution.

Yellen, J.L. May 1984. "Efficiency Wage Models of Unemployment." *American Economic Review* 74, pp. 200–205.

Zolas, N., Z. Kroff, E. Brynjolfsson, K. McElheran, D.N. Beede, C. Buffington, N. Goldschlag, L. Foster, and E. Dinlersoz. December 2020. *Advanced Technologies Adoption and Use by U.S. Firms: Evidence from the Annual Business Survey.* NBER Working Paper 28290.

About the Author

Martin Fleming is a Fellow of The Productivity Institute, a UK based research organization exploring what productivity means for businesses, workers, and communities, and a chief revenue scientist at Varicent, a Toronto-based sales-performance management software provider. Martin is also a researcher at the MIT–IBM Watson AI Lab and the U.S. Bureau of Economic Analysis.

Martin is the former IBM Chief Economist and former IBM Chief Analytics Officer. As IBM's Chief Economist, Martin provided regular macroeconomic insight and analysis to IBM's senior leaders and engaged with select IBM clients providing a view of the global economic outlook. Martin shared technology industry developments, insights, and forecasts with clients, industry professionals, academics, and policy makers.

Martin also led IBM's data science profession with the mission to drive the growth and expertise of IBM's skilled data science professionals, whose expertise will ensure success in the cognitive era.

As the chief analytics officer from 2010 to 2019, Martin led IBM's business model transformation initiatives employing machine learning, artificial intelligence, natural language processing in a cloud computing environment to improve decision making and, as a result, financial performance.

Previously, within IBM Corporate Strategy, Martin led IBM's Smarter Planet strategy development and execution with a focus on energy, climate change, transportation, water, and Smarter Cities.

Martin is a Fellow of the National Association for Business Economics (NABE) recognized for outstanding performance as a business economist, contribution to the field of business economics, and service to NABE.

Martin is a member and former chair of the Conference of Business Economists. Martin is a participant in the Brookings Productivity Measurement Initiative, organized by David Wessel and chaired by Janet Yellen. Martin was a member of the Federal Economic Statistics Advisory

Committee and a member of the Federal Reserve Bank of New York's Fintech Advisory Committee.

Prior to joining IBM, Martin was a principal consultant with Abt Associates, Cambridge, Massachusetts. He was also Vice President, Strategy for Reed-Elsevier, Inc., the Anglo-Dutch information company. Martin began his professional career at the System Dynamics Group, Alfred P. Sloan School of Management, Massachusetts Institute of Technology.

Martin holds a PhD and an MA in Economics from Tufts University and a BS *cum laude* in Mathematics from University of Massachusetts, Lowell.

Index

OTHER TITLES IN THE COLLABORATIVE INTELLIGENCE COLLECTION

Jim Spohrer and Haluk Demirkan, Editors

- *How Organizations Can Make the Most of Online Learning* by David Guralnick
- *Business and Emerging Technologies* by George Baffour
- *Teaching Higher Education to Lead* by Sam Choon-Yin
- *How to Talk to Data Scientists* by Jeremy Elser
- *Leadership in The Digital Age* by Niklas Hageback
- *Cultural Science* by William Sims Bainbridge
- *The Future of Work* by Yassi Moghaddam, Heather Yurko, and Haluk Demirkan
- *Advancing Talent Development* by Philip Gardner and Heather N. Maietta
- *Virtual Local Manufacturing Communities* by William Sims Bainbridge
- *T-Shaped Professionals* by Yassi Moghaddam, Haluk Demirkan, and James Spohrer
- *The Interconnected Individual* by Hunter Hastings and Jeff Saperstein

Concise and Applied Business Books

The Collection listed above is one of 30 business subject collections that Business Expert Press has grown to make BEP a premiere publisher of print and digital books. Our concise and applied books are for...

- Professionals and Practitioners
- Faculty who adopt our books for courses
- Librarians who know that BEP's Digital Libraries are a unique way to offer students ebooks to download, not restricted with any digital rights management
- Executive Training Course Leaders
- Business Seminar Organizers

Business Expert Press books are for anyone who needs to dig deeper on business ideas, goals, and solutions to everyday problems. Whether one print book, one ebook, or buying a digital library of 110 ebooks, we remain the affordable and smart way to be business smart. For more information, please visit www.businessexpertpress.com, or contact sales@businessexpertpress.com.

Lightning Source UK Ltd.
Milton Keynes UK
UKHW050233061022
409923UK00020B/1572